THE
Old Photographs
SERIES

LAWRENCE
TOWNSHIP

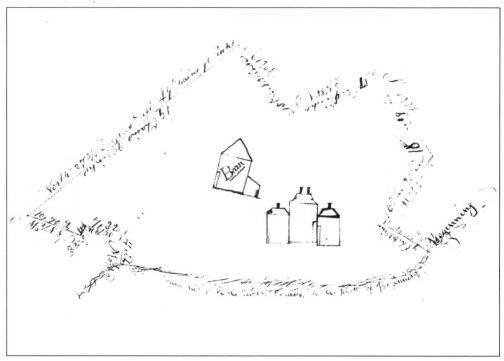

Mershon Map, March 3, 1737/8. Surveyors drew this map when Henry H. and Anne A. Mershon sold their farm to Peter Mershon (see page 4). Henry and Anne were among the earliest settlers in Lawrence Township, or Maidenhead, as it was then known. They arrived around 1700, when pamphlets advertised the area as having "rich fat soil" for farming, as well as "the healthiest aire" and "the goodliest woods." The sketches of the house and barn on the map, though not in scale, do record important details such as doorways and chimneys. The phrase at the bottom of the map, "Down the Creek the several Courses, to the place of Beginning," refers to the place where the Shabakunk branches from the Assunpink Creek. To the left, the "49 Chains, 90 links" on the western boundary refers to the size of the frontage on Lawrence Road. A "chain" was a surveying tool made of linked pieces of iron that measured 66 feet; each "link" was 7.92 inches. (Lawrence Township Archives)

THE
Old Photographs
SERIES

LAWRENCE
TOWNSHIP

Compiled by
Kathleen M. Middleton

**ALAN
SUTTON**

BATH • AUGUSTA • RENNES

First published 1994
Copyright ©Kathleen M. Middleton, 1994

Published by Alan Sutton, Inc., Augusta, Maine.
Distributed by Berwick Publishing, Inc.,
1 Washington Street, Dover, New Hampshire 03820.
Printed in Great Britain.

ISBN 0 7524 0068 1

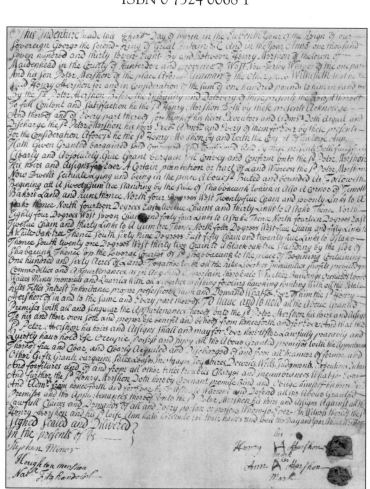

Mershon Deed, March 3, 1737/8. Signed during the reign of King George II with the marks "H" and "A," this deed conveys 160 acres of land in "Maidenhead in the County of Hunterdon and province of West Jersey" from Henry H. and Anne A. to Peter Mershon. In 1676, New Jersey was divided into the two provinces of East and West Jersey with Province Line Road forming part of the boundary between them. Although the Crown combined the two provinces into one colony in 1702, this deed suggests that the terms East and West Jersey remained in common usage even in 1737. Lawrence was part of Hunterdon County until 1838, when Mercer County was incorporated. The circles in the lower right corner are part of the original red wax seal. (Lawrence Township Archives)

Contents

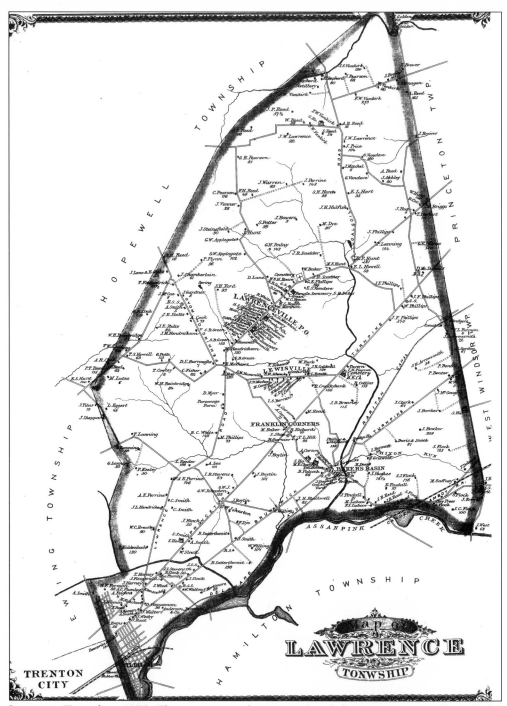

Lawrence Township, 1875. This map notes the name of each homeowner, as well as all the major buildings in the Township. Millham, in the lower left corner, was still part of Lawrence Township in 1875. In 1882 it became an independent township and then, in 1888, the eighth ward of Trenton. (*Combination Atlas*)

Map reference, 1875. This index identifies places that played critical roles in nineteenth-century daily life, such as mills, blacksmith shops, and stone quarries. The German translation was probably a popular feature of the atlas. Until the 1880s, when the "New Immigration" brought peoples from southern and eastern Europe to the United States, most immigrants were from either the British Isles or western Europe and spoke either English or German. (*Combination Atlas*)

Introduction

This book of photographs offers a visual history of Lawrence Township from 1865 to 1949. As these photographs show, the Township changed a great deal over that period of time. The one-room schoolhouses, the blacksmith shops, and the mills identified on the map on the opposite page have all but disappeared. The quiet, unpaved Brunswick Pike has been transformed into one of New Jersey's busiest highways, while the docks at Baker's Basin have lent their name to one of the state's largest inspection centers.

Despite these outward changes, the photographs also reveal a continuity between the past and the present. Looking at these photographs, we can recapture the pride of families gathering on their porches, as well as the nervousness of children posing for class pictures. We can readily identify with the people in these photographs precisely because of the continuity between their experiences and our own.

The ways in which these photographs present this tension between change and continuity is one reason they are such vital historical objects, for this tension allows us to explore how historical change has affected people in the past, and by extension, ourselves.

Kathleen M. Middleton
November, 1994

Acknowledgments

I am grateful to Mrs. Winona Nash, the Lawrence Township Historian, who helped me access the Lawrence Township Archives and patiently answered my numerous questions. Mrs. Nash has done an outstanding job collecting, preserving, and cataloging the various records and artifacts in the Lawrence Township Archives at the Mercer County Library. Over the years, various members of the Lawrence Historical Commission have assembled detailed records and manuscripts to document Lawrence Township's rich history. I have benefited from their work. Ms. Anne Kerr and her fine staff at the Mercer County Library Reference Department were invaluable during my research.

I owe thanks to Barbara Piscuscus and her staff at the Lawrenceville School Library for their assistance in finding, copying, and researching the history of the school. The staff of the New Jersey Room at the Newark Public Library was also helpful.

Many Lawrence residents assisted my research by opening their private photograph collections for me. Chief Nicholas Loveless allowed me to use photographs from his family collection, one of which serves as the cover for the book. Mr. Raymond Updike kindly provided me with the history of the Lawrenceville Presbyterian Church and his family, as well as photographs. Mr. and Mrs. Edgar Updike loaned me photographs and shared their memories of Lawrence with me. The Hullfish family, especially Bill and Gary, unearthed fascinating photographs and historical research for the book. Bill Hullfish also allowed me to use his family history manuscript, which includes a number of stories that he transcribed from family members over the years. Many of the photographs of the canal come from Donald Arrowsmith's collection of family photographs and artifacts. The Buxton family, especially Mr. and Mrs. Gordon T. Buxton, generously provided me with research on the Buxton Dairy, the Buxton family, and Clarksville. Mrs. Samuel Hamill graciously shared her photographs with me. Mrs. Dorothea Reed Pullen loaned me both her family photographs and her charming stories about Rosedale. Mrs. Lavinia Melton entertained me with her stories about growing up in the Township while allowing me to use her photographs. Miss Helen and Miss Viola Titus suggested many important areas of research as they shared their family photographs with me.

Finally, I must thank the Lawrenceville Presbyterian Church for allowing me to use their photographs, the Lawrenceville Fire Department for introducing me to many local historians, and the Lawrence Township Historical Society for sharing their resources with me.

Author's note: I have retained the original spelling and punctuation when quoting from manuscripts and letters. I have excluded photographs from World War II, because space did not permit an adequate treatment of this tumultuous period.

One
1865–1889

Cock and Bull Tavern, from a tintype, c. 1865. The people shivering on the back porch of this tavern at 2695 Main Street are probably members of the John A. Risdon family, who ran the tavern between 1860 and 1875. The census shows that John and his wife Margaret had five children in 1870: Benjamin, John, Joshua, Ella, and Ansetta. (Lawrence Township Archives)

Cock and Bull Tavern, from a tintype, c. 1865. This pre-revolutionary tavern has a long history. The earliest record of the tavern dates from 1789, when its owner, William Compton, applied for a tavern license. Compton probably did a good business at the tavern, because in the eighteenth century Main Street formed part of one of America's busiest roads, the King's Highway, which was the only major route between New York City and Philadelphia. Lord Cornwallis may have stopped at the tavern when he stayed in Lawrenceville during the Revolutionary War; when the tavern's owners found Cornwallis' diary in the attic years later, he had written, "One night in Maidenhead was more than enough." Besides being used as a tavern, the Cock and Bull also served as an early town hall. In 1816, residents met here to petition the state to change the Township's name from "Maidenhead" to "Lawrence" after the war hero Captain James Lawrence, who said "never give up the ship." Until 1890, most of the Township's elections and town meetings were held at the Cock and Bull, though not all of the Township's residents enjoyed having a tavern in the center of town. On May 8, 1853, George Phillips wrote in his diary that he was "pleased" that "the rum sellers license was taken away" from the tavern's owner, Mrs. Bashford. Phillips explained that drinking in the tavern "has ruined scores of persons I have no doubt. I always shun such contemptible places except on business such as state and Township elections, or business of some necessary publick nature." (Lawrence Township Archives)

Opposite, left: W.E.H. (1848–1909) and Elizabeth Fowler (b. 1820) Rouse, from a tintype, c. 1850. Right: Elizabeth Fowler Rouse, c. 1857. The daughter of Samuel and Nancy Fowler of Upper Freehold, Elizabeth came to Lawrence after her marriage to William Clark Rouse. On the left, their son William Edward Harper Rouse (see p. 20) sits in an infant's gown on her lap. Soon after this tintype was taken, the Rouses moved from the Cranstoun farm (see p. 52) to the "Rouse House" (see p. 70). Elizabeth's closely braided hair, taffeta ribbon, and knotted scarf or fichu in the picture on the right were all typical of pre-Civil War ladies' fashion. (Hullfish family)

The Smith farm, c. 1875. This farm was originally owned by the Mershon family (see p. 2). By 1870, Civil War veteran Charles Smith (b. 1845) and his wife Martha (b. 1847) owned it. Charles was a descendant of Joshua Smith, who bought the farm in 1757. The boy on the front porch may be Charles' son William (b. 1870). Lawrence Township's first mayor, Charles' grandson J. Russell Smith, was born in this house, today located on Getney Road. (Lawrence Township Archives)

"Elmwood," the residence of John Feaster Phillips (1829–1895), from a lithograph, 1875. When John married Hannah Ware in 1854, he received "Elmwood" as a wedding present from his father, Henry D. Phillips, a descendant of Theophilus Phillips who arrived in Lawrence as early as 1698. The women pictured riding sidesaddle and playing croquet could be John and Hannah's daughters: Jane, Elizabeth, and Anna May. Croquet was a fashionable sport in 1875, having been introduced to the United States around 1870. By 1895, John had increased "Elmwood" by 800 acres. After his death, his daughter Jane managed the estate. Although Jane (b. 1855), or "Jennie" as she was known, was raised as a nineteenth-century "lady" to play the piano and do fine needlework, she became well known as an excellent farm manager and owned the first tractor in Mercer County. Many residents recall seeing Jennie armed with a revolver driving a wagonload of milk to Trenton every morning. Mrs. Gertrude Scudder Bodine described Jennie to Donald Tyler as a "colorful character" whose "waves of laughter could rock a room." On the instructions of her physician, Jennie finally stopped doing cartwheels with the children around 1915. (*Combination Atlas*)

Lawrenceville School, from a lithograph, 1875. With just nine pupils, Issac Brown founded a private school in 1810, which he called "The Academy of Maidenhead." Around 1814, Brown built this building on 1 acre of land that he purchased for $25. It became known as "Hamill House" after the school's third headmaster, Samuel Hamill (see p. 16). It was Hamill who changed the name of the school to "Lawrence Classical and Commercial High School" in 1837. This lithograph shows the back of Hamill House as it looked from the southwest. To the far right are the clapboard, el-shaped additions that were placed on the northern end of the building between 1827 and 1857. (*Commercial Atlas*)

Lawrenceville School, from a lithograph, 1875. These fashionable carriages are driving down Main Street in front of Hamill House, the building on the right. The bay windows were added to the original stone front sometime after 1854. In front of Haskell House, to the left, several students are playing ball. (*Combination Atlas*)

Female Seminary, from a lithograph, 1875. James H. Porter built this girls' school at 2959 Main Street after leaving his teaching position at the Lawrenceville School. Porter died in 1834 on what was to be the school's opening day, but his widow finally opened the school in May 1835. In 1850, Dr. Charles William Nassau bought the school. In a November 1864 letter to her mother, Ella Elizabeth Reeder, a fourteen-year-old pupil boarding at the school, confesses that "I like Dr. Nassau a great deal better than I thought I would." The most interesting part of her letter concerns the presidential election of 1864 between the incumbent, Abraham Lincoln, and the war hero, General George B. McClellan. Because they doubted that Lincoln could end the Civil War (1861–1865), many Americans initially supported McClellan. After Union General W.T. Sherman won several victories in the Shenandoah Valley, Lincoln took the lead and won 212 of the 233 electoral votes. New Jersey voted for McClellen. Ella tells her mother that when "we heard that Lincoln was elected the girls were almost crazy. some of the girls had their feelings [hurt] very much. all the Lincolnites went out on the stoop and gave three cheers and made the Nassites very angry . . . I am very sorry that New Jersey went for [McClellen] but you would not expect anything else of it." (Lawrence Township Archives)

Lawrenceville Female Seminary.

The Graduating Class.

MARGARETTA E. BEAUMONT......................BROWNSBURG, PA.

MARY J. C. FARIES.................................WILLIAMSPORT, PA.

MARY P. HAMILTON.......... ....SPRUCE CREEK, PA.

MATTIE R. HUTCHINSON.....................BAKER'S BASIN, N. J.

MAGGIE A. McLEAN...............................WILKESBARRE, PA.

MARIA K. TORBERT............................... ....BROWNSBURG, PA.

KATE O. WHITE.............. ..................LAWRENCEVILLE, N. J.

WEDNESDAY, JULY 24th, 1867, 7 1-2 P. M.

ORDER OF EXERCISES.

Music,—La Traviata.

English Salutatory.......................................MAGGIE A. McLEAN

Music,—La Gallina.

Monumental Mounds of the Prairies........MARGARETTA E. BEAUMONT

Music,—Beautiful Doves.

Twilight of Our Being................................KATE O. WHITE

Music,—Il Nozze di Figaro.

A Gem from Life's Ocean, (A Poem)................MARY P. HAMILTON

Music,—Swiss Echo Song.

Enchantements Imaginaires.......................MARY J. C. FARIES

Music,—La Somnambula.

The Harp Untuned.................................MATTIE R. HUTCHINSON

Music,—Sisters, 'Ere we all are Parted.

Valedictory...MARIA K. TORBERT

CONFERRING OF DIPLOMAS.

PRAYER.

BENEDICTION.

MURPHY & BECHTEL, PRINTERS,

Female Seminary graduation program, 1867. The members of this graduating class would have been classmates of Ella Reeder, who wrote her mother that "there is only one nice girl in the room her name is Maggie Beaumont. she is one of my best friends." A few lines later she added that "Kate and I are great friends already." In the same letter, Ella also explained to her mother what a typical day at the school would have been like for these graduates. They rose at 6:00 A.M., said prayers, ate breakfast, and attended classes from 8:00 A.M. until 4:30 P.M., with a short break for lunch. This rigorous schedule would have been a surprise to George Phillips, who questioned the value of a seminary education in his diary on January 7, 1856. After lamenting that "the day of the good old customs of our fathers and mothers are fast passing away. Extinguished by the gaudy and superficial education bestowed upon our sons and daughters," George calls female seminaries "a mere humbug, a complete catchpenny, where parents pay extravagant prices for having their daughters half fed and their minds filled with the ostensible effect of display and promenade, in order to make them ladies and heads of families." Ten years later Ella Reeder would probably have disagreed with George that her seminary education was a "humbug." She wrote that she studied Biblical Antiquities, Latin Grammar, Astronomy, writing, reading, dictionary, and Algebra. Ella did, however, confirm George's view that the girls were "half-starved." She told her mother "if you had to eat all the hairs, worms, and flies that are found in the various things... one day one of the girls found a big white worm an inch long in her cabbage alive and the same day I found a fly or some kind of bug in my gravy and it is nothing to find hairs in almost anything." (*Commercial Atlas*)

Reverend Samuel M. Hamill, D.D. (1812–1889), 1875. A few years after Reverend Hamill and his brother Hugh became teachers at the Lawrenceville School, Reverend Hamill bought the school. Under his tenure, its enrollment and land-holdings grew enormously. In 1838, he wed the daughter of one of the original school trustees, Matilda Green. Mrs. Hamill helped her husband hold weekly socials for the students in their home; one student, Charles Scribner, became a famous New York publisher. Besides running the school, Reverend Hamill also developed a fine reputation as an orator. Many Civil War veterans said that they enlisted only after hearing one of his stirring pro-Union speeches. Dr. Hamill sold the school to the Green Foundation in 1874 and retired in 1883. (Woodward)

Dr. Abraham Gosman, D.D., c. 1885. Reverend Hamill (above) convinced Dr. Gosman to come to Lawrenceville from Princeton, where Dr. Gosman taught at the Theological Seminary. After his ordination in 1851, Dr. Gosman spent his entire ministry at the Lawrenceville Presbyterian Church and oversaw two church expansions. He was well-loved by the congregation. George Phillips records in his diary that on Christmas Eve, 1858, he and William Phillips called upon Dr. Gosman, as did "many of the congregation," to congratulate him on his marriage to Letitia Nassau, daughter of Dr. Nassau of the Female Seminary (see p. 14). After he retired in 1895, Dr. Gosman moved to "Twin Oaks" (see p. 55), where he lived until his death in 1899. (Lawrenceville Presbyterian Church)

Lawrenceville Schoolyard, c. 1880. Posed in their suits and hats, these Lawrenceville School students stand in the yard at the back of the school. The buildings, left to right, are the gym, Hamill House, and Haskell House. In the early 1880s, someone identified these buildings as "the Barn," the "Big House," and the "School House." (Lawrenceville School Archives)

Lawrenceville School baseball team, 1883/4. Lawrence Township boys began playing a form of baseball called "single and double cat" in the 1850s. In 1883, the school organized its first baseball team, which poses here outside of Green House. When the team played their first game on October 3, 1883, seven balls made a walk and batters could still call for a high or a low pitch. By 1940, the Schwartzkopf family lived at Green House, and the future General Norman H. Schwartzkopf played ball in this yard. (Hullfish family)

Mary Ellen Hullfish Applegate (1865–1942), *c.* 1885. The daughter of James M. and Margaret Long Hullfish of Franklin Park, Mary probably came to Lawrence when her sister Rosina opened a "tea room" on Main Street. Throughout the 1880s, fashion called for long jackets with dropped shoulderlines and knife-pleated skirts such as Mary is wearing. Dresses were made of upholstery-weight fabric and could weigh as much as 10 pounds. The bunched fabric under her left arm is part of the bustle of her skirt. (Hullfish family)

Marsh-White Home, *c.* 1875. These members of the Marsh family are pictured in front of their home on the north side of Lawrenceville Road near the Princeton border. The landscaping of the house is typical of the period. Until 1900, most people left the foundations of their homes visible rather than hiding them with shrubbery. Vine-covered porches, like this one, were quite popular after Andrew Jackson Downing, an influential architect and landscape artist, declared that a "broad shady veranda," or porch, "suggests ideas of comfort." (Princeton Historical Society)

Valley School, 1880. Huddled in the doorway on a dreary winter day is the entire student body of the one-room Valley School, which was located on the Princeton Pike near today's Texas Avenue. Miss Jennie Stults, the teacher, stands on the right next to the girls in the pinafores. The building to the left was the school outhouse; the barns to the far right were part of the Smith farm (see p. 11). The school property was also part of the Smith farm until William Smith donated land for the school to the Township in 1832. The Valley, or Red Brick, School was built entirely with such donations. When residents decided to replace the Oak Hill School on the Brunswick Pike, they sent out a handbill asking for subscriptions, arguing that a new school was necessary "considering the importance of English education to the rising generation." To keep building costs low, they took some of the bricks for the new 18.5 by 24-foot long building from the old Oak Hill School. When the Valley School opened in 1832, all the students up to the eighth grade sat at the continuous desk that ran around the four walls of the room. Some subjects, such as handwriting, were taught to all of the students at once. For other subjects such as reading, students from each grade took turns going to the center of the room where the teacher sat for their lessons. In 1880, the 12-foot wooden section shown above was added to the building, along with modern, free-standing desks. Even after the renovations, the school was heated with a wood stove. One day, some students climbed on the school roof and covered the top of the chimney for the stove. After smoke from the stove filled the room, the school closed for the day. (Lawrence Township Archives)

Hettie A. Rogers Rouse (1850–1911), *c.* 1888, and W.E.H. Rouse (1848–1902), *c.* 1885. After Hettie and W.E.H. were married on December 8, 1869, they had two children, Eden and Etta. The high-stand collar with lace trim on Hettie's dress was popular at the end of the 1880s. W.E.H.'s knotted cravat was a forerunner of the modern tie. (Hullfish family)

Eden Rouse (1870–1884), *c.*1875, and Etta Rouse (1881–1962), *c.* 1886. While Eden poses casually in a fashionable summer suit and striped stockings, Etta looks shyly at the camera in her delicate lace collar and cuffs. They both wear lace-up leather walking boots. Eden died during a severe scarlet fever epidemic while he was a student at the Lawrenceville School. The school yearbook notes his death and explains that the school closed for two weeks when the epidemic began. (Hullfish family)

Phoebe Ann Lee (1828–1908) and Vanroon (1820–1888) Rogers, from a tintype, c. 1875. Phoebe Ann and Vanroon were the parents of Hester Ann Rogers (opposite). Phoebe Ann holds the family Bible for this formal portrait. Her taffetta dress is typical of fashions after the Civil War, as is the lace cap covering her hair, which is looped and curled at the sides. Vanroon's long side whiskers and goatee were popular men's fashions in the 1870s. (Hullfish family)

Female Seminary, *c.* 1880. This view shows the seminary students and staff lined up on the back porch of the building. The two-story section to the right served as a dormitory for the girls. The clergyman standing on the porch could be Reverend Robert Hamill Davis, who ran the school for Dr. Charles Nassau from 1875 until it closed in 1883. The girls would not have been allowed to play unattended with the boys in the picture, because nineteenth-century etiquette dictated that boys and girls could socialize only under the watchful eye of a chaperone. Ella Reed explained to her mother in 1864 that although Dr. Nassau's nephew, Mr. Charles Nassau, was staying at the school, the girls were "not allowed to look at him or he at us." The seminary staff used special care to limit the girls' contact with Lawrenceville School boys. Ella wrote that during their afternoon walks, "we can only go as far as the church for Dr. Nassau will not trust us" to walk past the boys' school. On Sundays, the schools walked to the Lawrenceville Presbyterian Church at different times to keep the girls and boys from seeing each other in the street. Once inside the church, the boys sat in the balconies with the girls beneath them. Even so, Ella stated that the girls were "watched all the time" to see if they looked at the boys during the church service. (Lawrenceville Presbyterian Church)

Davis House, 1884/5. After the Female Seminary closed in 1883, the Lawrenceville School leased the building from the Davis family. It became known as Davis House after Reverend Robert Hamill Davis (see p. 22). The school made "Davis" part of the new House System, which was developed earlier in the century at the Rugby School, England, by Dr. Thomas Arnold. Under the House System, students were divided into small groups and placed in a home setting with a teacher and his family, rather than being boarded all together in large dormitories. The House System was one of the most important innovations of the John Cleve Green Foundation, which bought the school from Reverend Hamill (see p. 16) in 1879. John Green had been the youngest of Isaac Brown's original nine pupils (see p. 13). He left the bulk of the fortune he built from Chinese exports to the foundation, which in turn used the money to buy and expand the school. By 1885, the foundation had built five new "houses" in back of Hamill House. Pictured here in their bowler hats on the front steps of "Davis" are, left to right: (top row) house master James L. Patterson (in the chair), Halsey Hannahs, Hanson C. Stone (wearing a hat), and William W. Tyers; (second row) Alice Shewell, Maud Noble, Mrs. Noble (in the chair), Mrs. Patterson, "Billy" Breck in the arms of John M. Brook, and Walter Bowman; (third row, seated) Mrs. Breck, Arthur S. Walcott, "Joe" Patterson, Heatly C. Dulles (wearing a hat), Alexander S. Lilley (at Dulles' arm), William W. Tyers, and Fred E. Pierce; (fourth row) Edwin N. Whitfield, Conway A. Frost, J. Warren Bird, William S. Edey, Fred Santford (wearing a hat), T. Scott Brooke, Fred Ludlow (wearing a hat), and J. Chester McCoy (wearing a hat). In the front are George S. Wilkins, Chester C. Boynton (wearing a hat), and Delevan Pierson. (Lawrenceville School Archives)

Davis House, 1885/6. Seated in his silk top hat among the students on the back stairs of Davis House is the house master, Mr. James L. Patterson. His wife sits to his left. Like all house masters, James served as a surrogate parent for the boys. He was also responsible for running the household. The school gave him an allowance to pay the servants and buy the food, but he used his own funds to furnish the house. He seems to have been popular, if the way the students have gathered around him on the stairs is any guide. Among the students pictured are: Charlie Shoemaker, Henry Cochran, Albert Francke, E.H.L. Smith, Will Dinsmore, Fred Albree, Alfred Cook, Albert Cowin, John Fleming, Van Dyke Wight, Ernest Vanderburg, John Dwight, Charlie Bergen, John Sinclair, John Skinner, Bert Newton, George Butler, Herbert Smith, Gus Shepard, John Henderson, Theodore Hart, Victor Lewis, Dave Meeker, and Gardner Meeker. (Lawrenceville School Archives)

Haskell House, *c.* 1885. These workmen standing against the south side of Haskell House were probably completing the huge expansion project begun by the Green Foundation at the Lawrenceville School in 1882 (see p. 23). The original photograph is captioned "School Room Now Society Hall of JC Green Foundation." Dickinson House, one of the five Queen Anne-style Circle Houses built by the Green Foundation, appears on the far right. (Lawrenceville School Archives)

Cleve House, *c.* 1887. Many of these students posing with their lacrosse sticks in front of Cleve wear caps with the house colors, old gold and cardinal. Among the students are: John Fleming, Walter Stearns, Leroy Gresham, John and Henry Green, Ed Hamlin, Will Sexton, Norman McClintock, Dennis Michie, and George Acheson. Standing at the center are the house master, Dr. Howell Terry Pershing, and his wife. (Lawrenceville School Archives)

Thomas Branson DeCou (1849–1927), c. 1881. This formal portrait of Thomas, with his wide-roll collar jacket and watch chain, could have been taken for his wedding to Henrietta Lee (opposite) on March 3, 1881. The son of Samuel Ellis and Sarah Ransom DeCou, Thomas grew up in an eighteen-room house on Brunswick Avenue in Trenton that became the McKinley Hospital. (Raymond Updike)

The DeCou family, *c.* 1889. Thomas bought this home, Oakdale Farm, for his new bride, Henrietta Lee (1855–1941), the daughter of Randall and Francis Merschon Huchinson. They pose on the vine-covered front porch with their daughter, Edith, who was born on New Year's Day, 1883. Thomas was a pioneer in organizing Mercer County agriculture (see p. 107), and served in the State Assembly in 1903 and 1904. (Raymond Updike)

The DeCou family, *c.* 1889. The DeCous pose by the picket fence in the side garden at Oakdale Farm. The puffed sleeves on Henrietta's dress began to be fashionable in the late 1880s. By 1900, puffed sleeves had grown so large that women had difficulty getting through doorways while wearing them. (Raymond Updike)

Baker's Basin Canal bridge, c. 1880. The women standing on this bridge next to the Delaware and Raritan Canal are probably members of the James McGuigan family, who lived in the bridge-tender's house on the left. James McGuigan (b. 1835) was the bridge-tender at Baker's Basin for over twenty years. He immigrated to the United States from Ireland, as did his wife Bridget (b. 1836) and his mother Catherine (b. 1801). According to the 1870 census, his daughter Catherine would have been twenty-one in 1880. Like James McGuigan, many Irish immigrants in New Jersey found their first job with the Delaware and Raritan Canal Company. They initially worked digging the 66-mile-long canal bed by hand. Many of these workers died during a cholera epidemic at the construction site. After the canal opened in 1834, immigrants became canal walkers, checking the banks for erosion, or bridge-tenders, opening the canal bridges for passing barges. Lawrence had two other bridges over the canal, one at Carnegie Road and one at Port Mercer (see p. 80). This bridge was named for Benjamin Baker's boat basin, where barges often stopped to drop off coal, or to pick up lumber and produce from area farms. As barges approached the bridge, they signaled the bridge-tender by blowing on a conch shell horn. The bridge-tender, waiting in the small building on the right, would then push a shear pole to open the bridge and let the boat through. The "shear," a mechanism to lift heavy weights, was formed by the three posts rising around the women. The posts were joined at the top like a teepee, with weights suspended between them. As the bridge-tender pushed the shear pole, the weights would rise, and the bridge would open, as it appears in this picture. In 1880, over two hundred boats traveled past this bridge a day. At its peak between 1866 and 1871, the canal carried more tonnage than the famous Erie Canal in New York state. By the late 1880s, however, cargo was increasingly shipped by train. After 1892, the canal never showed a profit and it finally closed in 1933. (Lawrence Township Archives)

Two
1890–1899

Livery wagons, c. 1895. If Township residents or Lawrenceville School students wanted to go to places such as Trenton or Princeton, they could buy a ticket to ride there on one of these livery wagons, shown parked in front of Dickinson House. Besides running these passenger coaches, liveries also served as the nineteenth-century equivalent of rental car agencies by offering both horses and wagons for rent. In the 1890s, W.H. Applegate (see p. 32), Edmund Conover (see p. 43), Henry Bender, and Oliver La Rue all ran liveries in the Village. (Lawrence Township Archives)

Anne Knight (b. 1846) on the front porch of the Collins-Knight farm, *c.* 1898.

Edward C. Wood (1862–1900?) and
Ross Wood (1865–1900?), sons of
Anne Knight, in photographs taken
c. 1892. In her shirt-waist and
brooch, Anne Denby Knight
(opposite) relaxes on the front
porch of the Collins-Knight farm.
Anne came to the farm from Long
Island sometime around 1860 to
work as a servant for Edith and
Rachel Collins. The Collins sisters,
who listed their profession in the
1880 census as "ladies," had
inherited the Lewisville Road farm
from their father. Anne's three
children, two of whom are pictured
here, grew up on the farm. In 1868,
Anne married John DeKnight (b.
1840), a runaway slave who came to
the farm on the Underground
Railroad. Over the years, the
Collins sisters and the DeKnight
family became very close, and the
sisters paid for Anne's son Edward
to attend school in New York.
Rachel even willed her house, $200,
and 25 acres of her farm to Edward.
In 1888, Edward sold the farm to
Anne. After John's death in 1912,
Anne sold the farm to Susan D.
Pierson of the Princessville Inn.
Anne was known throughout the
Township as an excellent cook.
According to one of Anne's
relatives, Charlotte Boseley
Johnson (see p. 97), "Anne could
make 150 glasses of jelly a day."
(Lawrence Township Archives)

31

CORNER STONE LAYING!

The Corner Stone of the A. M. E. Church Mission, Louisville, near Lawrenceville, N. J., will be laid Sunday, July 26. Rev. L. W. Generette, the Pastor, is making preparations to have the frame up by that time.

Several prominent divines are expected to be present. Among them are Revs. J. C. Ayler, P. E.; J. T. Diggs, J. W. Cooper, Wm. Middleton, H. H. Pinckney and Bishop H. M. Turner, D. D., LL. D.

Preaching at 11 A. M., and at 2.30 P. M. the coner stone will be laid.

The public is invited to attend these services. If stormy, the next fair day.

Mt. Pisgah A.M.E. Church handbill, 1890. Reverend L.W. Generette prepared this handbill to advertise the opening of the Mount Pisgah A.M.E. Church on Lewisville Road. Before the church opened, black families met for church services on Sunday mornings in each others' homes. The head of the house conducted the service and then the families ate Sunday dinner together. After the congregation hired Reverend Generette to preach, they built a one-room church that held sixty people. W.A. "Cap" Furman and his daughters Caroline and Anne (see page 59) came each week to teach Sunday school lessons to the children. Some of the original members of the church were the John DeKnight family (see p. 31), the Samuel Duncan family, the Theodore Schenck family (see p. 156), the Pierce family, and the Jordon family. The first babies christened in the church were Georgianna Schenck and Sheldon Jordan. Charlotte Bosley and Sheldon Jordon had the first wedding in the church. (Lawrence Township Archives)

William H. Applegate (1863–1924), c. 1895, and Archibald G. Hullfish (1880–1945), c. 1895. "Bill" Applegate owned one of the busiest livery stables in Lawrenceville (opposite). His high-buttoned suit, bow tie, and long mustache were popular men's fashions in the 1890s. After Bill married Mary Hullfish (see p. 18), he hired his brother-in-law "A.G." Hullfish as a driver for his livery. In the portrait on the right, A.G. looks very much the young gentleman in his high-stand collar and knotted tie. After driving for Applegate's livery, he started several businesses, such as the Lawrenceville Ice and Coal Company (see p.153). (Hullfish family)

Applegate Livery Wagon, *c.* 1895. Advertising "W.H. Applegate, Lawrenceville" on its black leather top, this wagon is parked behind Applegate's store (see p. 36) in front of the barn where Bill housed the horses and wagons for his livery. Applegate's sold tickets for passengers to ride to Trenton and back in this wagon which left Lawrenceville for Trenton twice a day, at 7:30 A.M. and 1:30 P.M. Before returning to Lawrenceville, it stopped in Trenton at the United States Hotel at 10:00 A.M. and 4:45 P.M., and at the Pennsylvania Railroad depot at 10:10 A.M. and 4:55 P.M. If it was raining, passengers could roll down the side curtains. Since Applegate's served as a branch of the Adam's Express Company, this wagon carried mail, packages, and trunks for delivery in Lawrence and Trenton, as well as passengers. The baggage and large packages fit in the rack around the top, the trunks on the rack in the back. The livery's advertising slogan was "Errands promptly attended to." When Bill's brothers-in-law A.G. and Jimmy Hullfish drove the stage, they made the nearly two-hour trip to Trenton twice a day. In the summer, the road was dusty. In the winter, the ride was cold. In the spring, the road was muddy. The road to Trenton was not much better in 1895 than in 1830 when William Cobbett, the English writer and social reformer, wrote that the "roads of New Jersey, between Trenton and Elizabeth-Town, at the breaking up of winter" were the worst he had ever seen. (Lawrence Township Archives)

Coach and four, *c.* 1892. Jimmy Hullfish (see p. 42) captured these three scenes of a tallyho stopping at Applegate's to change horses. Once the carriage stopped, the grooms unhitched the horses while the passengers stepped out of the carriage to stretch their legs, as above. The scene was a familiar one at Applegate's, because carriage horses needed to be changed every 14 miles. Even so, the boys on the left seem to be enjoying the excitement. (Hullfish family)

Changing horses, *c.* 1892. After the horses were unhitched, they were led down this alley to the livery barn in the back of Applegate's store. Fresh horses from livery were then brought up the alley and hitched to the carriage. The men gathered on the porch probably owned these four horses, which have saddles and stirrups for individual riders. If the men went inside, they could tie up their horses to iron hitching posts like the one in the foreground. (Hullfish family)

Coach and four, *c.* 1892. While the driver restrained the fresh horses, the passengers got back into the tallyho to continue their trip up Main Street. The building in the rear is Stone Cottage. The telephone pole at the center of the picture dates from 1884, when Furman's store (see p. 62) installed the first pay phone in the Village. In 1892, there were still only four phones in the Village, all with one digit phone numbers. (Hullfish family)

Applegate's Livery, 1898. This boy holds the reins for a horse hitched to the Applegate delivery van, which is parked in front of the livery barns behind Applegate's store. (B. Bentley)

Applegate's porch, *c.* 1898. These women seem to have taken a break from their reading to enjoy a soda in the late afternoon sun on the porch of Applegate's. They could be Bill Applegate's two daughters, Edith and Ada, who would have been nineteen and sixteen in 1898. A boy riding a bicycle has just passed a carriage parked in front of the store. The helping hand sign on the right reads "W.T. Applegate's Livery Stable," which was down the alley to the left. Hamill House stands across the street on the far right. (Lawrence Township Archives)

Main Street, *c.* 1895. This view of Main Street is taken from the entrance of the Lawrenceville School. A bicycle leans on a tree in front of Stone Cottage, the first building to the left. The flags are raised in front of Applegate's store, where the Applegate delivery van is parked. Further up Main Street, a boy riding his bike has turned to look over his shoulder at the camera. (B. Bentley)

Applegate's fountain with William A. Hullfish (1878–1957), 1895. Until he enlisted in the army (see p. 59), "Bill" Hullfish worked for his brother-in-law Bill Applegate. In this picture, Bill poses in his knotted cravat and white jacket behind the soda fountain in Applegate's store. One can easily imagine him pouring a soda for his brothers A.G. and Jimmy when they finished driving the Applegate stage to Trenton each afternoon (see p. 33). Behind Bill are a variety of candies, baked goods, and ice cream. Some of the signs read "Don't Monkey with Imitations," "Velvet: America's Favorite Candy," "Uneeda Biscuits," "Uneeda Jinjer Wagfers," and "United Ham." Like other store-owners (see p. 46), Bill Applegate used the parasols hanging on the right to decorate the store until some lady bought them to protect her delicate complexion. Bill later decorated the ceiling with carved table tops. Each year, he prepared a soft wooden top for the graduating class of the Lawrenceville School. It became a rite of passage for each boy to go to Applegate's and carve his name on the table. When the store closed in 1920, over twenty carved table tops were hanging from the ceiling. (Hullfish family)

Cleve Select Driving Club, c. 1897. These four Lawrenceville School students pose with their coats and canes as "The Cleve Select Driving Club." They are, left to right: the masters Howard, Turner, Gaylord, and Dempster. They seem to be sitting on a bed in a hallway of Cleve House; a pillow and mattress ticking are just visible at their sides. The sign to the left is an advertisement for Applegate's Livery. (Lawrenceville School Archives)

Arrival at Woodhull, 1894. On the right, masters Breckenridge and Bell carry their baggage into Woodhull after arriving at the Lawrenceville School in a livery wagon. In back of the wagon is Dickinson House. The buildings in the distance are part of the Lawrenceville Presbyterian Church. The trees were planted in the 1880s as part of the landscaping done by Frederick Law Olmstead, "the father of American parks." (Lawrenceville School Archives)

Woodhull, 1894/5. In this formal house portrait, about half of the students wear their hair parted down the middle and combed with pomade in the new 1890s hairstyle. House master Arthur Lee James, his wife, and his son stand in the center of the back row. Some of the students are: House President William Shell, Albert Moller, M.C. Greeley, and Thomas Adams. This building was the second Woodhull House, built immediately after the original burned in 1892. (Lawrenceville School Archives)

Thanksgiving table, c. 1895. Mrs. MacKensie, the headmaster's wife, was known for the elaborate feasts that she planned for students who could not go home on holidays. Even the school yearbooks took note of these events. Here, the Davis dining room has been lavishly decorated with garlands, ferns, and carnations for the holiday meal. (Lawrenceville School Archives)

Dickinson House group, 1895/6. Instead of going to bed after the night bell rang at 9:30 P.M., many Lawrenceville School students played well into the night, like the boys pictured here. Sometimes, the students even climbed through windows to play outside, which explains why so many of these boys are wearing shoes with their pajamas. The boy in the silk top hat and bow tie in the front row is Owen Johnson (1878–1952), who gained fame for the school and himself with his comic stories of school life. Johnson graduated at the age of sixteen in the class of 1895, but he returned for one postgraduate year to help launch a new magazine, *The Lawrenceville Lit* (see p. 47). After he graduated from Yale, his Lawrenceville stories were published in magazines such as *The Saturday Evening Post*. They were so widely popular that they were turned into books such as *The Prodigious Hickey* (1908), *The Varmint* (1910), and *The Tennessee Shad* (1911). In 1949, Metro-Goldwyn-Mayer made a movie based on the books (see p. 159). Throughout these stories, Johnson's characters get in and out of trouble, devise plans to annoy their teachers, worship their athletic heroes, and generally do anything but study. All of his characters enjoy night parties, for as one narrator asks, "What gorging dinner party could compare with the thrill of feasting at midnight on crackers and cheese, deviled ham, boned chicken, mince pie and root beer by the light of a solitary candle, with the cracks of the doors and windows smothered with rugs and blankets." (Lawrenceville School Archives)

Opposite, top: "Musicians at Midnight," 1893. With a variety of clothes thrown over their pajamas, the members of this quartet happily entertained their Cleve housemates well into the night. The musicians are: Adolph E. Bone (strumming the guitar in the front), Stacy B. Lloyd (harmonizing with the bottle and tin pail on the left), Charles Johnson (rapidly fingering his guitar in the back), and John B. Adams (plucking the mandolin on the right). (Lawrenceville School Archives)

"A Card Game," Cleve House, 1893. Only one of these card sharks can tear his eyes away from his hand to look at the camera for this picture. The players are, left to right: Henry Church, George T. Lambert, Lindsley Haviland (with pipe), and Norman De Mauriac. (Lawrenceville School Archives)

Lawrenceville School class, 1895. Owen Johnson based all of the central characters in his stories on his classmates. The students identified with numbers above are: 1) Franklin Carter; 2) Noel Fox; 3) William Heron, "The Tennessee Shad"; 4) P. Wentz,"King of the Kennedy"; 5) Joshua Butler Wright, "Butsey White"; 6) Marshall Geer; 7) Owen Johnson; 8) Middleton Beaman; 9) W.O. Hickok, "The Prodigious Hickey," who won first prize in public speaking. Johnson used Hickok as the model for "The Prodigious Hickey," who "with face as innocent as a choir boy's," "planned the revolts against the masters, organized the midnight feasts and the painting of watertowers." In the stories, it is Hickey who dreams up the nicknames for his classmates. Johnson calls the nickname that Hickey created for William Heron, the "The Tennessee Shad," Hickey's *magnum opus*." As the narrator explains, the name conveys the Shad's "incredible, preposterous boniness such as could only have been possessed by that antediluvian monster that did or did not sharpen its sides on the ridges of Tennessee." When the Shad walked, he was "like a pair of animated scissors," for "his coat hung from the points of his shoulder blades as though floating from a rake." Although the Shad turned laziness into a fine art, "he liked nothing better than to propose ideas . . . to throw out suggestions that would produce commotions and give him the keen intellectual enjoyment of watching others hustle." (Hullfish family)

Lawrence Cameron Hull, c. 1897. Sitting in his study is the Lawrenceville School Latin teacher, the "Old Roman." In the stories he becomes "Lucius Cassius Hopkins, "The Roman", man of heroic and consular mold, flunker of boys and deviser of systems against which even the ingenuity of a Hickey hurled itself in vain." Elsewhere, the Roman seems like the "watcher of the galley slaves in *Ben Hur*." Despite his intimidating appearance, "The Roman" proves to be "The Varmint's" greatest friend. (Lawrenceville School Archives)

Emma "Auntie" Conover (1833–1929), c. 1898. Emma stands smiling on the front porch of her home, which her parents John and Betsey Scudder bought in 1841. She and her husband Edmund Conover (1833–1919) ran a livery in back of this house at 2705 Main Street. They also opened a restaurant in a small room at the front of it. As the narrator of *The Prodigious Hickey* explains, "Conover's was not in the catalogue that anxious parents study, but then catalogues are like epitaphs in a cemetery. Next to the Jigger Shop, Conover's was quite the most important institution in the school. In a little white Colonial cottage, Conover, veteran of the late war, and Mrs. Conover, still in active service, supplied pancakes and maple syrup on a cash basis." It is at Conover's that "Little Hungry Smeed" eats forty-nine pancakes. By doing so, he forces the Conovers to fulfill their promise of free pancakes for everyone if any boy, "at one continuous sitting, unaided, should succeed in swallowing the awful number of thirty-two" pancakes. (Lawrenceville School Archives)

Lawrenceville School Football Team, 1895. Many of the plots in Johnson's stories involve the school's favorite sport, football. As a student, Johnson cheered for this team, whose members were, left to right: (standing) Davis, Street (coach), Argersinger (manager), Edwards, Cadwalader, and Eddy; (seated) Fred W. "Cap" Kafer, Emerson, Righter, and Dibble; (kneeling) Richards, Powell, and Simons. (Hullfish family)

Condit Woodhull Dibble, c. 1895. By 1892, football players were so adored by the school that the special football issue of the school paper gave biographies of each player on the front page. Condit was one of the team's outstanding players and the model for Johnson's character "Flash Conduit." He also held the school record for the 100-yard dash (10 seconds) for over ten years. "The Varmint" thought "Flash Conduit" "greater . . . than the faint heroes of mythology." Condit wears a typical football uniform for the 1890s: soft trousers, a padded shirt, and heavy boots. Helmets and shoulder pads were not used until well after 1900. (Hullfish family)

Spot and Bill Orem (1827–1907), *c.* 1895. Spot and Bill look seriously at the camera as they sit outside Bill's home next to Haskell House on Main Street, where they lived with Bill's wife May (b. 1832) and his daughter Susan (b. 1858). For over thirty years, Bill ran a shoemaker shop on the side of the house. Since Bill repaired baseballs and footballs as well as shoes, he was well-known by Lawrenceville School students, who enjoyed listening to the tall tales that he told as he worked in his shop. Bill figures in Johnson's stories as "Bill Orum." Spot seems to be the model for Bill Orum's dog, Henry Clay, who had "certain marks that would permit him for purposes of classification to be described as a setter." In Johnson's story, Bill Orum boasts that Clay "could annihilate anything that attacked him on the *left* side; the right eye having glorious gone in a victorious career." To emphasize how much Bill Orum has exaggerated the dog's prowess, Johnson's narrator has Al Bogart describe Henry Clay a few pages later as a "walleyed setter whose teeth have to be tied in." (Donald Arrowsmith)

House League Championship Football Game, *c.* 1898. With an anxious crowd behind them, these teams prepare for the next play on the field next to the old gymnasium and the power house-electric plant building. The Dickinson House team won the game. (Lawrenceville School Archives)

45

"Al" Bogart presiding in the Jigger Shop, c. 1895. Jiggers at Dewitt's Drugstore on Main Street were a Lawrenceville School institution. The origin of the term "jigger" is unclear, but one of Johnson's narrators explains that "A jigger is unlike any other ice cream. It is dipped from the creamy tin by a cone-shaped scoop called a jigger, which gives it an unusual and peculiar flavor." The narrator laments that the "original jigger has been contaminated and made ridiculous by offensive alliances with upstart syrups, meringues, and macaroons with absurd titles, but then the boy went to the simple jigger as the sturdy Roman went to the cold waters of the Tiber." In 1895, a jigger cost 5¢; a double jigger cost 10¢. Hungry Smeed's first triumph is to eat ten double jiggers. Although Civil War surgeon Dr. Edmund Dewitt and his wife Eleanor owned the store, they wisely allowed Alfred "Al" Bogart (b. 1876) to run it for them, for as one of Johnson's narrators regretfully explains, "Al made no errors, his sympathies were deaf to the call, and he never (like the doctor) committed the mistake of returning too much change." As in the picture above, Al mans the counter in Johnson's stories as the "Guardian of the Jigger," "a creature without heart or pity" who could not be tricked into giving jiggers away. His "abnormal taste" for Spencer's *Faerie Queene* "made him absolutely incomprehensible to the boyish mind." (Lawrenceville School Archives)

The *Lit* Board, 1896. Owen Johnson, the managing editor, sits second from the left with the staff he assembled to found the *Lawrence Lit*. The other members of the board are: the business manager, D.D. Tenney, and associate editors E.C. Douglas, C.W. Dibble, D.B.S. Rathburn, R.A. Rice, G.M. Shepherd, and R.V. Look. (Hullfish family)

Croquet, *c.* 1898. These boys are practising their croquet swings in front of Foundation House, the headmaster's residence built by the Green Foundation for the MacKensie family. The man in the straw boater on the left is probably James Cameron MacKensie, head master from 1883 to 1901. (Lawrenceville School Archives)

J.E. Hullfish, Athletic Goods, 1898. James "Jimmy" Edward Hullfish (see p. 96) opened this store on Main Street with his brother Peter around 1895. The baseball trousers on the table were called "knickerbockers," or "knickers," after the New York baseball team that adopted them as part of their uniform in 1849. The shelves on the right hold bicycle supplies, while the glass counter contains boots, shirts, and socks. (Hullfish family)

J.E. Hullfish, Athletic Goods, c. 1898. Outside the store, four boys examine tandem bicycles. Jimmy Hullfish had the first pneumatic bicycle in town, which he rode to the Chicago World Fair in 1892. The Hullfishs rented bicycles for 20¢ an hour, or $1.50 a day. During the bicycle craze of the 1890s, they probably did a brisk business. Windmills like the one in the center were used throughout the Township to draw water from wells. (Hullfish family)

Prize-winning photograph, 1898. The pictures on pages 49 and 50 are taken from an album owned by J.V.A. MacMurray, a Lawrenceville School student. On the inside cover of the album, entitled "Blue Prints of and about Lawrenceville," MacMurray wrote that "the album was won by Ralph Charles Edward Musar and J.V.A MacMurray in the Photographic Contest held by J.E. Hullfish in the spring of 1898: Second prize." Jimmy Hullfish became an avid photographer after buying his first camera in 1892. This photograph of the brook near Lawrence Station, won second place in the contest. (Lawrenceville School Archives)

Old Shanty, 1898. This photograph from the MacMurray album shows a small cider mill shanty. It could be the one that Donald Tyler mentions as being on the Vancleve Homestead, on Lawrenceville Road next to the Davis House. (Lawrenceville School Archives)

Top: Blacksmith's Shop, 1898. MacMurray labeled this picture "Arthur Forger in the Blacksmith's Shop near the Davis House." R. Burrough Scudder (b. 1828) owned this shop between 2895 and 2909 Main Street. Here, the smith heats a horseshoe over the fire in the forge until it is soft enough to bend into the shape of a horse's foot. Blacksmiths were critical to a farm community like Lawrence, because horseshoes were easily damaged or lost on dirt roads, and farmers depended on horses to do various farm chores. Smiths also made tools such as hammers, scythes, and ploughs. (Lawrenceville School Archives)

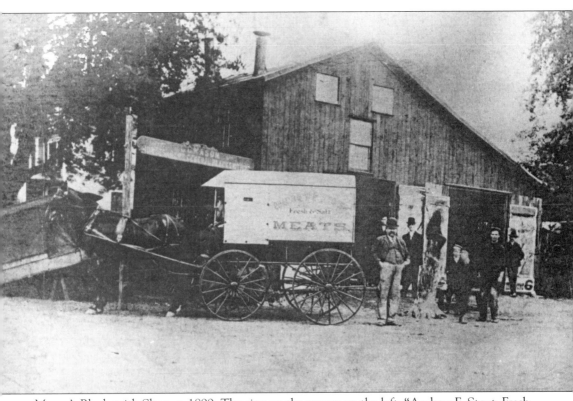

Mason's Blacksmith Shop, c. 1899. The sign on the wagon on the left, "Andrew F. Stout, Fresh and Salt Meats," refers to Andrew F. Stout (b. 1861) who listed his occupation in the 1900 census as "huckster." He used three of these huckster wagons to sell meat from his slaughterhouse to area residents. Huckster wagons traveled the streets of Lawrence well into the twentieth century (see p. 128). In the days before supermarkets, or automobiles, people welcomed the chance to buy things such as meat, hardware, or clothing without traveling an hour to do so. Customers also enjoyed hearing gossip and area news from the hucksters. The sign on the shop in back of the wagon reads: "C.C. Mason, Horses and General Blacksmithing." Clarence C. Mason (b. 1876) took over this blacksmith shop on the Brunswick Pike in 1898 when he married Susan B. Slack (b. 1879), whose father Joseph (1843–1888) opened the shop around 1870. Joseph and his wife Ella (b. 1849) moved here from Doylestown, Pennsylvania, after the Civil War. The area around the shop soon became known as "Slackwood" after Joseph and his friend William Wood, a potter who immigrated to the United States from England in 1869. William's wife Anne (b. 1843) followed him in 1870, and they moved to Lawrence in 1873. Around 1880, Joseph and William each bought land and built houses which they sold to workers in the Millham potteries and the Hamilton Rubber Works. The area, the first planned suburban development in Lawrence Township, quickly grew from twelve households in 1874 to forty-five households in 1897. By 1904, the suburb had grown so large that the Township built the Slackwood School for the children in the area. (Lawrence Township Archives)

Opposite: Blacksmith's Shop, 1898. Having heated the shoe, the blacksmith now hammers it over the beak of the anvil until it takes the shape of the horse's hoof. After testing the fit of the hot shoe on the horse, the smith would adjust the shoe's fit, punch nail holes into it, and then nail the shoe onto the hoof. The blacksmith may be Thomas B. Stout (b. 1863), who was listed in the 1897/8 Trenton Directory as the blacksmith in Lawrenceville. (Lawrenceville School Archives)

The Cranstoun family at "Hedgerow," c. 1897. John D. Cranstoun (1854–1945) and his wife Jennie (b. 1861) moved to this farm on Lawrenceville Road in 1894. John stands in a felt trilby hat in the center. With a baby in her arms, Jennie stands in back of the hammock to his left. According to the census, the Cranstoun children were: Adam, Robbie, William, Susie, John, Charles, George, and Leroy. (Princeton Historical Society)

Left: Emily Hutchinson DeCou (1885–1964), c. 1898. Emily's high-stand collar and puffed sleeves were fashionable in the late 1890s, as was the narrow band of pleated fabric, called ruched trim, on her shoulder. Right: Arthur (1888–1974) and Sarah (1892–1984) DeCou, c. 1896. While Arthur stands serenely in his suit and silk bow tie, Sarah looks somewhat apprehensive, despite her pretty white dress and baloney curls. Like Emily, Arthur and Sarah were the children of Thomas and Henrietta DeCou (see p. 27). (Raymond Updike)

Left: Boy with dogs, *c.* 1896. This unidentified young member of the Hullfish family seems quite at ease on the porch between his dog and his puppy. Right: Etta Hullfish Rouse, *c.* 1894. Etta sits amid mountain scenery in a pretty dress with a pleated front, plaid fabric trim, and puffed sleeves. (Hullfish family)

Cracker and Whiskey House, *c.* 1898. Jimmy Hullfish (see p. 96) took this photograph of his brother Peter's home at 2431 Main Street. The name dates from the eighteenth century, when the owner avoided buying a liquor license by including a free drink with the purchase of a few crackers. (Hullfish family)

Interior of Lawrenceville Presbyterian Church, 1898. The flowers and trimmings mark the 200th anniversary of the church. The earliest record of the church is a deed dated March 18, 1698, that grants 100 acres (the "town lot") to the inhabitants of Maidenhead for a meeting house, cemetery, and school. (Hullfish family)

Lawrenceville Presbyterian Church and brick chapel, 1898. To the right of the church is the brick chapel, built in 1898 to replace the Session House. The two men stand on a long wooden platform to the side of the chapel. Parishioners stepped onto the platform when getting out of their carriages so that their long skirts and good shoes would not get covered in mud. People on horseback tied their horses to the hitching post on the right. (Hullfish family)

"Twin Oaks Farm," *c.* 1898. Known also as "The Birches" and "The Old Mansion House," this farm was willed by Jasper Smith III to the Presbyterian Church in 1813. The church used it as the manse until 1899, then leased it to George R. Cook, the manager of a rubber mill. The Lawrence Municipal Building now stands on this site. (Lawrenceville Township Archives)

Children at Twin Oaks, *c.* 1899. The farm became known as Twin Oaks after an American patriot hid behind these trees during the Revolutionary War to spy on British patrols passing along the King's Highway after the Battle of Trenton. These could be the children of George and Mary Cook: Ellanor, Horace, and Donald. (Lawrenceville Township Archives)

Lawrenceville Dramatic Club, May 27–28, 1898. The club poses in costume on the stage at Memorial Hall during its hit production of William Gillette's *The Private Secretary*. Some of the cast members are: Harland C. Nicholson, Hugh Herndon, Rufus Parks, Jr., Franklin Abbott, Stanley Bright, M. Maclay Alden, Houston L. Gaddis, Fritz Behr, Houston L. Gaddis, and Ernest Van Tassell. (Lawrenceville School Archives)

Lawrenceville Dramatic Club, 1898. This formal cast picture for *The Private Secretary* shows John D. Turner on the left in the checked suit he wore for his role as the Bond Street tailor Sidney Gibson. Robert E. Russell sits on the right in the wig and spectacles he wore as Mr. Cattermole. Given that the female roles were all played by boys, this picture is a testament to the costumer's art. (Lawrenceville School Archives)

Staff of Upper House, 1896. The kitchen and house staff are assembled outside of Upper House, the residence for fourth year students. In Johnson's stories, staff members frequently serve as accomplices to the boys' schemes, as when the waiter Klondike Jackson spies on the Kennedy House boys for Hickey. (Lawrenceville School Archives)

Davis House, c. 1897. The books and papers on this table in the house reading room suggest that students will be returning to study any minute. The students often enjoyed playing the pump organ to the left during their study breaks. (Lawrenceville School Archives)

The Arrowsmith family, *c.* 1898. The James and Abigail Arrowsmith family lived on a farm near Port Mercer (see p. 80). Their children were, left to right: J. Clark, Theodore L., John , and Francis (see p. 89). In the front sit Elizabeth, George, and Aunt Eliza Arrowsmith. This portrait was taken just before George went south to improve his health. (Helen and Viola Titus)

Captain William and Philip Sheridan Bilbee, *c.* 1898. Captain Bilbee wore his original Civil War army uniform and hat for this portrait, taken when his son Philip entered the United States Navy. Many Township students met Captain William Bilbee when he visited their schools on Memorial Day to tell them about the Civil War. (Lawrence Township Archives)

William Arthur Hullfish (1878–1957), 1898. Bill poses in the army uniform that he wore during the Spanish-American War. Bill often said that he walked home after being discharged from the service in the Midwest. (Hullfish family)

Furman House, c. 1895. Peering through the first floor window seems to be Mary Furman (b. 1851), whose husband Nathanial Higgins Furman (b. 1838) bought this house on 2719 Main Street in 1869. The people standing on the porch are probably Mary's mother, Louisa J. Howell (b. 1826), and Mary's daughter, Louisa Ruth (b. 1889). (Hullfish family)

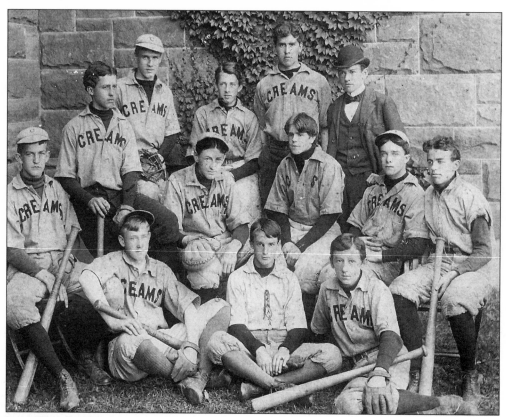

Lawrenceville Creams, *c.* 1898. The School baseball team poses in their team shirts, knickerbockers, hose, and leather boots outside Haskell House. The team may have used the "hit and run" play, developed in the 1890s, against their opponents. (Lawrenceville School Archives)

Track day, 1899. The men in their straw boaters sit next to the ladies with their parasols on the edge of the track field. The two boys sitting on the left are playing catch between events. (Lawrenceville School Archives)

Opening day of the Trenton Street Railway Company trolley, 1899. Throughout the spring of 1899, Township residents watched eagerly as the tracks for the first trolley were laid along the southeast side of Lawrenceville Road. The opening day festivities began at noon on June 15, 1899, when a contingent of three trolleys stopped at Trenton City Hall so that railway, city, and county officials could give speeches and board the cars. Then the cars started for Lawrenceville as the music of Winkler's Band drifted from the first car. All along the tracks, people waved flags at the cars, which were decorated by S.P. Dunham and Company with flags and bunting in the Lawrenceville School colors, red and black. To area farmers, the sight was astounding. Instead of horses pulling wagons past their farms, three electric cars were gliding down the street. Around 2:00 P.M., a huge crowd cheered as the first trolley car reached the gate of the Lawrenceville School, which had excused its students from classes for the celebration. As the Trenton notables got off the cars, school students and Township residents scrambled aboard them for this picture in front of Hamill House, which Peter Hullfish turned into a postcard. Peter's son, Raymond Hullfish, sits atop the trolley on the left. (Lawrence Township Archives)

Main Street, c. 1899. This turn-of-the-century view of Main Street shows a horse-drawn sleigh parked on the left and trolley car No. 140 riding up Main Street on the right. These numbered trolley cars ran down the street every forty minutes from 6:00 A.M. to 12:00 A.M. The trolleys ended the rural isolation of the Township, because they could bring people to and from Trenton in less than an hour for only 20¢. In 1902, the Johnson Trolley Line, called "The Fast Line" opened another route on the northern side of the Township. Despite the convenience of the trolleys, horse-drawn sleighs were still the easiest way to travel in the snow, since trolleys frequently lost their electrical power during snowstorms or stalled on snow-covered tracks. The sleigh above is parked in front of Nathanial Furman's store. Furman began running the store in 1868, continuing a tradition that began in 1821 when Ralph Shreve opened a store here. Many Lawrenceville School boys bought books for their classes and furniture for their rooms at Furman's. Since Furman's housed the Village post office, Township residents used it as an informal town center. The newly built Kafer Flats can be seen behind Furman's. (Lawrenceville School Archives)

Three
1900–1910

Valley School, *c.* 1900. The students pose with the American flag, the girls in their pinafores on the left and the boys in their suits on the right. Miss Jennie Stults, their teacher, sits authoritatively in the center. In 1905 the Valley School closed, having been replaced by the Slackwood School (see p. 75) and the Lawrence Elementary School. (Lawrence Township Archives).

Upper House, 1900. As the elected officers of Upper House, the senior class residence, these boys were completely in charge of discipline in the house. Pictured above are Directors Charles N. Glover, John R. DeWitt, and George Shedden, as well as Associate Directors Nathanial Higgins, William F. Damon, and Chase Williams. (Lawrenceville School Archives).

Griswold House, c. 1901. After classes ended at 3:05 P.M., Lawrenceville School students had three hours of free time before dinner at 6:20 P.M. Here, they use their time to walk, sit, bicycle, and compare notes in front of Griswold House. (Lawrenceville School Archives)

Quarantine, *c.* 1901. During a quarantine for scarlet fever, the residents of Davis House kept themselves busy by staging a play, *Mrs. Jarley's Waxworks*. Some of the cast members pictured above are: C.H. Raymond, Frederich Somerville, Horace Pomeroy, John Steen, Frank Wright, and Charles Moore. (Lawrenceville School Archives)

Baseball game, *c.* 1901. The band members have paused in adjusting their music to watch one player clear first base, as his teammate runs towards third. (Lawrenceville School Archives)

Dickinson House, 1901. Some of the students posing for this house portrait are: Dudley Willcox, George L. Forsyth, L.W. Moore, Willard Barton, John F. Rust, James W. Gillis, S.A. Halsey, Henry B. Darlington, G. Douglas, Albert Potter, A.W. Markhouse, P. Wells, L.M. Buck, Frank Gornell, P. Welles, Harry Habermare, Clark Carson, Lemuel Osborne, Albert K. Smiley, Alex Milne, and R.S. Cook. (Lawrenceville School Archives)

Foundation House, c. 1901. This view of the sitting rooms shows the MacKensie family's piano in the corner of the room to the right. Pianos and book-covered tables, like the one on the left, could be found in many nineteenth-century homes. In these days before television, families gathered in the evenings to listen to music and to look at picture books. Through the open door in the rear is the headmaster's study. (Lawrenceville School Archives)

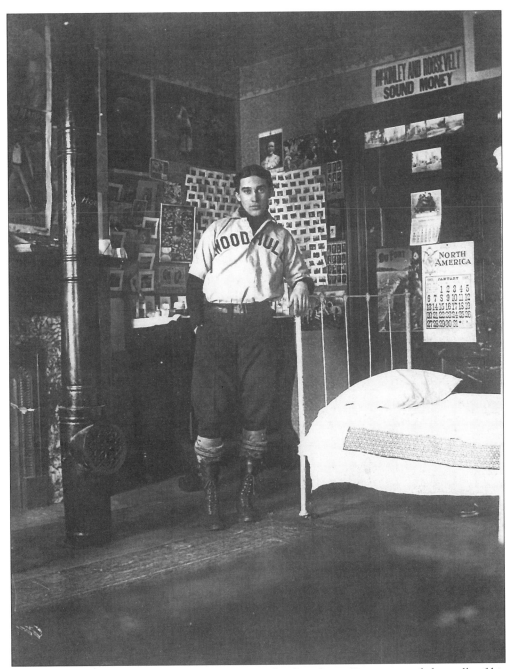

Dean R. Good, 1902. Like most Lawrenceville School students, Dean covered the walls of his room with pictures and posters. The poster over the door, "McKinley and Roosevelt: Sound Money" dates from the 1900 presidential campaign. After being re-elected, largely because of his support for prosperity and the gold standard, William McKinley was assassinated in September 1901, and his vice-president, Theodore Roosevelt, became president. The pipe to the left was part of the intricate central heating system in Woodhull. (Lawrenceville School Archives)

Etta Rouse, 1902. This lovely portrait was taken for Etta's wedding to A.G. Hullfish at the Rouse farm on November 2, 1902. Bill Hullfish and Ada Bussom were best man and maid of honor; Kathleen and Margaret Applegate were flower girls. The pintucks and gathered sleeves on Etta's dress were fashionable at the turn of the century. (Hullfish family)

The Rouse family, c. 1906. The friends and family of W.E.H. and Hettie Rouse have gathered in their finest clothes on the front porch of the Rouses' home for this picture. In the second row to the far left is Etta Rouse Hullfish. Behind Etta is Ada Bussom, her closest friend. To Etta's left sit her parents, W.E.H. and Hettie Rouse. Seated to the left in the top row is Phoebe Ann Rogers, Hettie's mother. The woman with her face half hidden beside Phoebe Ann is her sister, Elizabeth Rogers. Leaning toward the camera at the far right of the second row is Jimmy Hullfish's wife, Mary or "Mae." After Etta wed A.G. Hullfish, Mae became her sister-in-law. Directly to Mae's right sits her mother, Mrs. Lizzie R. White Howell. (Hullfish family)

Rouse farm, *c.* 1905. This view of the house from Lawrence Road shows a tree-cutting scene. Ever the gentleman, W.E.H. Rouse stands at the center in a straw boater, white shirt, and vest, with a crowbar in his left hand. (Lawrence Township Archives)

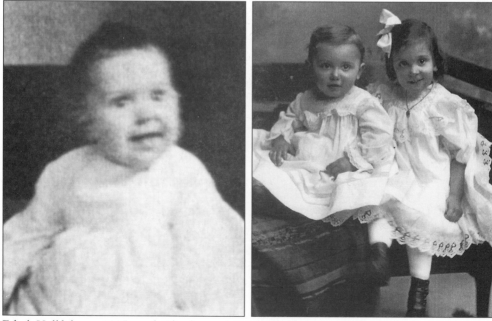

Ethel Hullfish, *c.* 1905, and Charles and Ethel Hullfish, *c.* 1907. Ethel (b. 1904) seems mesmerized by the camera taking her baby picture (left). Just a few years later (right), she poses prettily in her silk bow, lace dress, locket, and buttoned shoes with her brother, Charles (b. 1905).

Applegate children, *c.* 1902. Standing in front of Bill and Mary Hullfish Applegate's store are their children, left to right: Kathleen (b. 1894), Leroy (b. 1896), Louisa (b. 1895), James Clifton (b. 1900), Margaret (b. 1893), and Mary (b. 1904). Their brother George was born in September 1905 (see p. 141). The store entrance was on the left, under the "Hancock's Ice Cream" sign. (Lawrence Township Archives)

Bill Applegate, *c.* 1903. Standing in front of his store in his suit and bowler hat, Bill looks very much as Owen Johnson described him, a "quick businesslike little man with a Western mustache" and "a general air of being on the trigger." The Applegate family lived on the right side of the twenty-two room house and used a doorway under their front stairs to enter the store. Bill Hullfish (see p. 145) recalls that as a child the Applegates' library was the only place that he ever saw so many books. (Hullfish family)

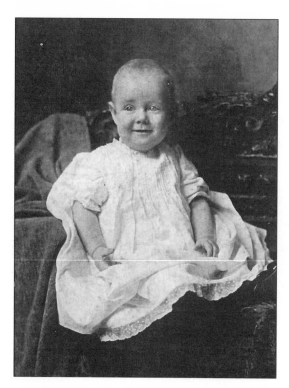

Thomas Blackwell Reed, 1907. Family legend holds that Thomas, the son of Francis Johnson and Martha Ann Golden Reed, was born with a tooth in his mouth. Certainly, this picture proves that Thomas (b. February 1907) was a big baby. (Dorothea Reed Pullen)

Private school, 1904. Miss Tilden, the teacher, is surrounded by her class at 2810 Main Street, where she ran a small private school. The young children in the front row seem too excited to stand still. The board and batten siding on the building behind the class was popularized by Andrew Jackson Downing in the mid-nineteenth century. (Lawrence Township Archives)

Haying, *c.* 1907. In a field on his Bunker Hill Road farm (see p. 104), Frank Ketterer (1870–1918) stands atop the haywagon packing the hay that his brother, in the foreground, throws up to him. Standing on a haywagon was dangerous, because if the horses moved, Frank could have easily fallen off the wagon or onto a pitch fork. Once the wagon was full, Frank would have taken the hay to a barn for storage. Hay had to be stored quickly to keep dew or rain from ruining it. (N. Loveless)

Left: Hay storage barns, *c.* 1902. If a farmer could not get his hay into the barn quickly, he devised coverings such as these portable barns to keep it dry. This type of four-pole barn originated in Holland. By the 1900s, farmers used tarpaulin rather than the traditional thatch for a roof. (Lawrenceville School Archives) Right: Frank Ketterer, *c.* 1908. Frank stands next to his horse in his farmyard. The slat siding on the corncrib in back of him prevented spoilage by allowing air to circulate around the corn. (N. Loveless)

Theresa Ketterer, c. 1907. Frank Ketterer's daughter, Theresa, sits holding a calf. The girl on her left is a relative, probably a cousin. Farm children were frequently given chores such as tending calves, milking cows, or chopping wood. (N. Loveless)

Gathering flowers, c. 1907. Theresa Ketterer leans on the fence holding a handful of daisies. Although farm life could be difficult, open fields did provide opportunities for gathering flowers and making daisy chains. (N. Loveless)

Slackwood School, 1905. The Township built this two-room school for $3,725 to serve the growing suburb of Slackwood. Even in 1905, Slackwood was a rural community, and many of its students lived on farms. A boy who lived on the farm across the road from the school had the chore of feeding the family pigs. One morning, he forgot to feed them. As the pigs became hungrier and hungrier, they began to squeal. By mid-morning, the pigs' squealing could be heard so loudly inside the school that none of the children could concentrate on their schoolwork. The teacher, Mabel Updegrove, let the boy go home to feed the pigs. (Lawrence Township Archives)

Slackwood School, 1905. This class was the first to graduate from the Slackwood School. In the center of the back row stands the teacher, who not only taught all the grades, but also took care of the coal furnaces. After the Valley School closed, Miss Stults became the teaching principal at Slackwood at a salary of $49.50 per month. (Lawrence Township Archives)

Elwood Morris (b. 1886), c. 1905. As part of his job at Mason's blacksmiths shop, Elwood prepared horses' hooves for shoeing, as he does here. He used the hoof parer in his hands to trim the hoof so that the shoe would fit smoothly. In the foreground, a shoeing hammer rests in a nail box. Elwood lived in Slackwood with his parents, Peter and Jane Morris. (Lawrence Township Archives)

Slackwood, *c.* 1907. Mason's blacksmiths shop is on the right, looking much as it did in 1899 (see p. 51). Across Brunswick Avenue from Mason's is the Nash home. On the left are the Jone's Grocery Store and the Feed Store. In the foreground is Valley Forge Avenue. (Lawrence Township Archives)

The Nash family, 1906. Standing in front of their home are, from left to right: James (b. 1890), Mary E. (b. 1872), Herbert (b. 1868), and John (b. 1891) Nash. Alice (b. 1893) stands on the porch holding the dog. Herbert immigrated to the United States from England in 1886. He worked as a tile presser in the nearby potteries, as did James. Alice became a teacher and ultimately the principal of school No. 4. (Lawrence Township Archives)

Slackwood engine house, 1907. Most of the community seems to have attended this flag drill in Slackwood. The girls with the sashes and flags stand in front of the firehouse, which was built and run by volunteers. (Lawrence Township Archives)

CONSTITUTION

OF THE

Slackwood Shooting & Pleasure Association,

OF

SLACKWOOD, N. J.

1905.

TRENTON, N. J.:
S. Mellor. Jr. & Son, Book and Job Printers.
1905

Slackwood Shooting and Pleasure Association, 1905. One measure of Slackwood's growth is the development of organizations in the area, such as the fire department and the Shooting Club. The club owned a chicken coop near Harmony Avenue that it used as a clubhouse. When the club disbanded in 1913, it sold the building to the Board of Education for use as a school. (Lawrence Township Archives)

The Arrowsmith family, c. 1903. After meeting in Clarksville, John A. and Anna Mercer Cubberly Arrowsmith were married on March 8, 1896. They pose with their family in the home they rented on the John E. Gordon farm in Port Mercer. Behind the sofa stand Fannie (b. 1897) and John. Seated, left to right, are Carrie (b. 1899), Raymond (b. 1897), and Anna (b. 1872). Anna holds Walter (b. 1902) on her lap. Ray and Anna have their eyes squeezed shut, while the others seem startled by the flash of the camera. The "print holder" on the wall behind them folded out to store lithographs, etchings, or important papers. Like the other furnishings, the print holder was delivered to the Arrowsmiths by a freight steamer on the canal. (Donald Arrowsmith)

Port Mercer Canal bridge, *c.* 1905. The shearpole bridge has opened to let the tugboat *Relief* pass. This company boat traveled the canal twice a month to pay bridge- and lock-tenders. By 1905, barges unloaded much of the coal used throughout the Township into the storehouse for Mather's General Store on the left. (Donald Arrowsmith)

Port Mercer Canal bridge, *c.* 1905. In this view, the Port Mercer Canal bridge has closed so that wagons and horses traveling on Quakerbridge Road can cross the canal. On the far left is Mather's General Store. The building with the picket fence to the right is the bridge-tender's home, now the site of the Lawrence Historical Society. Port Mercer was named for General Mercer, who died in 1777 after being wounded in the Battle of Princeton. (Donald Arrowsmith)

John Arrowsmith, *c.* 1907. John sits enjoying a cigar next to the buttonwood tree in front of the bridge-tender's home at Port Mercer. After working as a manager on the J.F. Phillips farm (see p. 12) and farming part of the J. Gordon property, John became the bridge-tender at Port Mercer around 1905. In the background to the left is Mather's store. (Donald Arrowsmith)

Clarksville School, 1905. Like other children from Port Mercer, the Arrowsmith children attended the Clarksville School (opposite). Their teacher, Bertha Seely, is seated on the right in the first row. Ray Arrowsmith is in the second row, standing third from the left. His sister Carrie stands on his right. Fannie Arrowsmith is in the third row, fourth from the right. In the back, third from the right, is William Owl, an Indian from Carlisle, Pennsylvania, who worked on the West family's Brunswick Pike farm. After he returned to Pennsylvania, he played football with Jim Thorpe. Also in the back row are Stella Cook, Southerd Mather, and John Robbins. Some of the other students are: Lillie Haverstock (Ray Arrowsmith's future bride), Grace Everitt, Eden West, Etta Belle Mather, John Mather, Wardell Seely, and Harry Kelly. The Mathers were all children of Charles Mather, who owned the general store at Port Mercer. Etta Belle Mather later became a teacher at the Clarksville School. (Lawrence Township Archives)

Clarksville School, c. 1908. The Arrowsmith children walked to this one-room school on Quakerbridge Road each morning. On their way, they passed the small village of Clarksville, which had a blacksmith shop, a store, a hotel, and a saloon. Once they arrived at the school, they hung up their coats and put away their lunch pails in the small vestibule at the front of the building. The pole rising on the roof was a lightning rod. (Lawrence Township Archives)

Two Clarksville School pictures, c. 1909. The young man on the left seems disgusted with his sailor suit, the wicker chair, and the photographer's directions. The girl on the right poses in her starched pinafore with one of the new crankless telephones. The only telephone in the area at the time was at Mather's store. (Donald Arrowsmith)

CLARKSVILLE
PUBLIC SCHOOL
District No. 4
—o—
Lawrence Twp., Mercer Co., New Jersey
—o—
MISS BERTHA SEELY, Teacher
—o—
Pupils

Wardell Seely	John Mather
Russell Coleman	William Dooling
Jesse Powlas	Louis Merricks
James Dooling	Lester Brady
Jasper Allen	Harry Kelley
William Golden	Raymond Arrowsmith
Jay Bross	Alfred Berrien
Henry Doherty	VanKirk Silcox
Harold Golden	Harry Dooling
Levell Kirchner	Leroy Hawke
Wesley Updyke	Elmer Updyke
Leroy Coleman	Christian Effinger
Walter Arrowsmith	Samuel Johnson
Joseph Trinchiski	Willie Wilburton
Ellsworth Schenck	Margaret Haverstock
Stella Cook	Eva Kirchner
Merta Cook	Lillian Haverstock
Fannie Arrowsmith	Jeannette Dooling
Victorine Doherty	Sarah Golden
Mabel Bross	Hattie Effinger
Carrie Arrowsmith	Marian Coleman
Elsie McBrien	Katie Wilburton
Mary Trinchiski	Mary Golden
Ola Everett	Hannah Johnson
Helen Berrien	Gladys Pierson
Ethel Vanarsdale	Emma Haverstock

—o—
School Board

Mr. H. D. Cranston	Mr. Clark Flock
Mr. Chas. H. Smith	Mr. Frank Carr
Mr. E. C. Seely	

Clarksville School souvenir, 1908. Like most teachers, Miss Bertha Seely gave each of her pupils a small gift at the end of the school year. Walter Arrowsmith saved this booklet from 1908. The first page reads "In memory of days spent together in the schoolroom, this token is presented with the compliments of YOUR TEACHER." The last page (bottom) lists all the students in the school. The cover (top) serves as a reminder of American cultural values at the start of the century. With the portrait of George Washington, the flag, and the American eagle, the cover is unabashedly nationalistic. The globe at the center hints at America's new role as a world power. The schoolbooks, paper, and inkwell on the left take on a patriotic significance in this setting, so that one is tempted to reword the motto "Education is Wealth" as "Education is National Wealth." In fact, as America moved from a rural to an industrial nation, education took on a new importance. In the nineteenth century, most Americans accepted Horace Greely's maxim that farming was the "best business" and had taken his advice to "Go West, young man." By 1908, the American ideal had shifted from cowboys to the heroes of Horatio Alger's novels who went to the city, worked hard, and "got ahead." As Alger's heroes learn, "getting ahead" in an industrial world was impossible without reading, writing, and math skills. By 1908, then, education had become critical for the strength of the nation, as this cover suggests. (Lawrence Township Archives)

Clarksville Sunday school, *c.* 1908. The Arrowsmith children line up for this picture with their friends after Sunday school. Like the other one-room schools in Lawrence, the Clarksville School served as a non-denominational Sunday school on weekends. For many years, Clark Arrowsmith was the Sunday school teacher in Clarksville. (Donald Arrowsmith)

Morris Hall, *c.* 1905. Morris Hall opened as a residential home for the aged in 1905. The brick building with beautifully carved Gothic oak wainscotting was built by Bishop McFaul of Trenton. Until the Morris Hall Chapel was built in 1910, Roman Catholics walked or took the trolley to Trenton to hear Mass. (B. Bentley)

William Tilton (1884–1964), 1906. "Bill" was the son of Clarence and Bertha Tilton. In his twenties he gained local fame as the manager and second-baseman of the 1906 champion Waldron baseball team. After marrying Edith DeCou (see p. 27), he served as the first Township Tax Collector for thirty-three years. (Raymond Updike)

Lawrenceville Post Office, c. 1907. Seen from the center of Main Street, the signs on the front of Furman's store read, left to right, "Lawrenceville Post Office," "N.H. Furman and Sons," and "John L. Stout's Sporting Goods Store." William Austin Furman, Nathanial's son, stands second from the left. Peter Coffee's pressing shop was in the rear of the building. (Hullfish family)

Amos Bosley (1851–1941), c. 1909. Born to Amos and Sarah Bosley in Bensalem, Pennsylvania, Amos left home at age eight to become a "bound boy" on a Pennsylvania farm. After working as a shoemaker and a coachman, he came to Lawrenceville in 1903 to help his wife's cousin, Anne Knight (see p. 97). After 1908, Amos began working at Golding and Bogart's (below). He became a favorite of the Lawrenceville School students, who used to rub his shaved head for luck. (Lavinia Bosley Melton)

Golding and Bogart, c. 1910. Around 1908, Dr. Dewitt sold his drugstore, known informally as "The Jigger Shop," to Warren Golding, who then became partners with Al Bogart (see p. 46). In 1911, New Jersey Governor Woodrow Wilson outlawed public cups, such as those next to the cut glass punch bowl on the counter, for health reasons. (Lawrenceville School Archives)

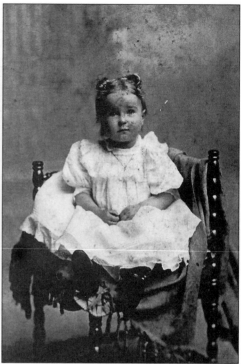

Helen A. Titus (b. 1903), *c.* 1903, and Viola M. Titus (b. 1906), *c.* 1906. With their blond curls and charming lace dresses, these sisters are the image of girlhood at the turn of the century. They lived with their parents, William A. and Francis Arrowsmith Titus, on a farm at the corner of the Princeton Pike and Darrah Lane. (Donald Arrowsmith)

Slackwood School, *c.* 1910. In this school picture taken on the side of the school, the Titus sisters sit in the front row surrounded by their classmates. Helen sits third from the right; Viola sits ninth from the left. Both sisters eventually became teachers. (Helen and Viola Titus)

Edith Applegate Taylor, 1910. The graceful folds of Edith's dress are typical of fashions around 1910, which moved away from the lace and puffs of 1900. The day of her wedding, her five-year-old brother George disappeared. After most of the Village turned out to look for him, someone found him sleeping in the doghouse behind the Applegate home. (Hullfish family)

Mill at Lawrence Station, *c.* 1910. Between 1905 and 1920, the area around Baker's Basin and Youngs Road held a $135,000 a year business complex. One of the largest businesses in the area was the Howell and Sons' Flour Mill on the Assunpink Creek, pictured above. Helen and Viola Titus (see p. 88) remember riding in their father's wagon to bring grist to the mill, where it was ground into feed or flour with a water-driven stone grinder. Other businesses in the area were John H. Bahrenburg's Natural Ice Plant (see p. 127) and J.H. Allen and Sons' Grain Thrashers and Coal Dealers. Isaac Taylor was the local blacksmith, and Stephen McGuigan the local wheelwright. At Conover and Allen's General Store, people bought tickets for the train station (opposite) that gave the area its name. (Lawrence Township Archives)

Lawrence Station, c. 1910. These men are waiting for a train at the Township depot on Lawrence Station Road. E.E. Seely, a member of the Township Board of Education, was the station agent and postmaster; Samuel Hunter was the flagman. The original station was located in Baker's Basin and called "Hutchinson's Station" after Gideon Hutchinson, who opened a general store there in 1831. After the station was moved east around 1867, it was renamed "Lawrence Station." (Lawrence Township Archives)

Track workers, c. 1910. These men stand to the left of the Lawrence Station depot. The man with the crowbar sixth from the left is Mr. Colavita. Track workers walked the track daily, pounding the rails into shape and shoveling stone along the line. (Lawrence Township Archives)

This tugboat is pulling a barge laden with steel down the canal, c. 1909. This tugboat is pulling a barge laden with steel down the canal. By 1909, barge traffic had almost disappeared on the canal, because most manufacturers found shipping their goods on trains to be cheaper than shipping them on barges. Trains also ran all winter, whereas ice forced the canal to close for several months of the year. (Lawrence Township Archives)

Martha Ford (left) and Edna May Pierson, later Mrs. Harry Bilbee, proudly hold this hunting dog in the backyard of the Pierson home on Cherry Tree Lane, c. 1910. (Lawrence Township Archives)

92

Left: Mary I. Nash, *c.* 1910. In her pompadour and shirtwaist, Mary sits on a fence next to the canal and aims her box camera at the photographer. (Lawrence Township Archives) Right: Poise, *c.* 1910. This woman wears the headband, sailor's shirt, and knickers that Paris fashion designers recommended for balancing on a rock next to the canal. (Donald Arrowsmith)

These children are watching a yacht, the *Green Goose*, coast down the canal near Slackwood, *c.* 1920. As barges stopped using the canal, pleasure boats began using it for cruises. (Lawrence Township Archives)

Brunswick Pike, 1910. The boy and girl in the center are walking south towards the tree line of the Shabakink Creek. The land to the right and left of the road was known as "Steven's Meadow." The Brunswick Pike was paved and renamed "Route 1" a few years after this picture was taken. (Lawrence Township Archives)

Steven's Meadow, c. 1910. This detail of a larger photograph shows a young lady standing in the eastern side of the meadow, her arms filled with wildflowers. (Lawrence Township Archives)

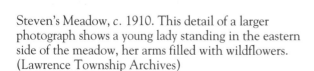

94

Four

1911–1920

Bill Applegate behind the wheel, *c.* 1915. Bill poses at the wheel of his new-fangled automobile while his granddaughters giggle in the back seat. As in many cars built before 1925, the steering wheel is on the right side. Cars were a rare sight in the Township until after 1912, when low prices made cars available to most families; between 1911 and 1920, the number of registered cars in the United States multiplied more than eight times over. Like the trolley, cars ended the rural isolation of the Township by making commuting to and shopping in places such as Trenton convenient. (Hullfish family)

A Hullfish family reunion, 1911. The entire Hullfish family has gathered on this porch, along with their friends the Bussoms, the Rules, the Griggs, the Applegates, and the Clarks, among others. Margaret Long Hullfish, the matriarch of the family, stands in the doorway in the back row. (Hullfish family)

James Edward "Jimmy" Hullfish (1872–1958), 1911. This detail from the photograph above shows Jimmy Hullfish, who became the model for the livery driver in the Owen Johnson stories after he started working for Bill Applegate in 1892 (see p. 33). In a wonderful scene at the opening of *The Varmint* Jimmy, the "connoisseur of new arrivals," bites his lip to keep from laughing while Dink Stover tells outrageous lies to "The Roman" (see p. 43). Students enjoyed riding with Jimmy, for as Johnson's narrator explains, he never minded the way they "clustered on the top like bees on a comb of honey." After opening a store with his brother Pete on Main Street (see p. 48), Jimmy introduced running water to the Village by installing an electric motor to pump water into a wooden, 1,000-gallon storage tank behind his home. Later, he helped found the Lawrenceville Water Company. (Hullfish family)

The Anne and John DeKnight family, c. 1912. Soon after her cousin Anne Knight bought the Collins' farm (see p. 31), Charlotte Demby Bosley and her husband Amos moved from Pennsylvania with their three daughters, Frances, Charlotte, and Florence to help the Knights run the farm. Having been born in the city, the Bosley children were overwhelmed by the Lawrence countryside. Amos' daughter Charlotte Jordan (b. 1899) recalls that the "first thing about moving here was I looked up and saw the sky. I never saw so much sky. And the sunrise! The moon, we were just about afraid of it. The sky was so fierce." Within a few years of the move, the Bosleys' children Lavinia and Allen were born. At the family gathering on the farm pictured above, Henry Freemont (left, kneeling) shows the group how to build a fire Indian style. Gathered around the fire are, left to right: Frances LeCompt (daughter of Amos); Lemuel Campbell; Lavinia Thomas (sister to Amos); Clarence Demby (brother to Charlotte); Amos (seated); Allen (in front of Amos); Florence Turner, Lavinia Melton, and Charlotte Jordan (daughters of Amos). Anne Knight (with the hat) and Charlotte Bosley sit on the far right. After Anne sold the farm in 1913, the Bosley's moved to Lewisville Road, where they enjoyed parading with drums and costumes on the Fourth of July. Other times, they would race two-wheeled wagons pulled by their dogs. Charlotte Jordan recalls that the day the cow died, "we walked to school and just sat and cried. The teacher said 'You'd better go home where you'd be more comfortable.'" (Lawrence Township Archives)

The Salt family, 1914. On the front porch of their Merline Avenue home are, left to right: John Millwood Salt, Anne Dorothy Salt Bayless (b. 1911), and Alma Grace Bauer Salt. (Lawrence Township Archives)

The Salt family summer camp, c. 1914. These men are relaxing in front of the Salt bungalow, which John Salt's brother built on land that he leased along the canal. John Salt's family joined his brother at the bungalow for several weeks each summer to swim and fish along the cooling breezes of the canal. (Lawrence Township Archives)

Skating on the canal, *c.* 1908. The couple on the right has stopped ice-skating to watch the children play on the canal near today's Whitehead Road. While the boys in the center enjoy sledding on the ice, the other children skate. Many Township children enjoyed skating on the canal and then going to stores along the canal for hot cocoa. Ray Arrowsmith (see p. 79) recalled skating all the way to Trenton for a date. (Lawrence Township Archives)

The Dettman family, *c.* 1917. Seated in the yard of their Slackwood home are Elizabeth, George, and Ethel (b. June 1901) Dettman. Ethel became a well-known teacher in the Lawrenceville Schools and won the Township's first Citizen Award. (Lawrence Historical Society)

An Arrowsmith family portrait, c. 1913. In their chrysanthemum boutonnieres and lace dresses, the Arrowsmith family poses next to the Port Mercer bridge-tender's house. Family tradition holds that John planned this portrait as a surprise. When the photographer appeared, Anna had to scramble to dress the children. In the back row are, left to right: Ray, Fannie, Carrie, and Walter (see p. 79). In the front row stand William (b. 1911), John, George (b. 1905), Anna, and Clark (b. 1905), nicknamed "Dink" after the comic strip character P.B. Dink. William, on the left, died four years after this picture was taken. After he disappeared one afternoon, the entire neighborhood searched for him until dark. That night, his father John dreamt that William was on a sandbar. There was a sandbar beneath the bridge where a drain from Quakerbridge Road emptied into the canal. The next morning when John dove into the canal at the base of the bridge, he found William dead. An Indian working on a nearby farm had taught most of the children to swim, but William had never learned how. (Donald Arrowsmith)

Arrowsmith and Ferrand children, c. 1911. The Arrowsmith family made a number of friends when boats stopped at Port Mercer to stay overnight or buy food at Mather's store. This picture forms the front of a postcard that is inscribed: "The *Eva II* is now in her winter quarters awaiting better weather. Present our best regards to your mother and father. Signed Ed Ferrand, Bound Brook." (Donald Arrowsmith)

Boat No. 1, c. 1911. Carrie Arrowsmith stands to the far left of the deck on this houseboat, which is tied to the dock at Port Mercer with the ropes in the foreground. Fannie Arrowsmith, at the far right, holds up her doll for the camera. Like most boats at the time, this one signaled the bridge-tender with a steam whistle. George Arrowsmith recalled that the first time they heard a boat use a siren, the whole neighborhood panicked; animals squalled and children cried. Many residents thought the noise came from a wild animal and ran towards the canal with their guns. (Donald Arrowsmith)

A trolley stalled on Main Street, 1914. After several severe storms in February 1914, Lawrenceville was hit with at least a foot of snow and ice on March 1 and 2. In places, the drifts were 5 to 7 feet high. This trolley car was stuck in the snow without power for several days. The trolleymen could not leave the car unattended, so they took turns going to local farmhouses for food. Since the whole Village was without electricity, Jim Hullfish ran his water pumps (see p. 96) by hooking them up to his car's motor. Some Lawrenceville School students became local celebrities by "displaying the prowess of pioneers," as the *Trenton Evening Times* phrased it. A March 3, 1914 *Times* story explains that the day before, two students, Dick Ryan and Phil Kauffman, had walked through snow "neck deep" from Lawrenceville to Trenton to win a bet of $50 offered by other members of the Upper House. The only people they saw the entire way to Trenton and back were four other Lawrenceville School students: George Weldon, captain of the football team, John Wolf, captain of the hockey team, Laster Tyrell, and Earl Hayden. Whereas Ryan and Kauffman took three hours to make the trip, this second group made it in a "record" two and a half hours. (Lawrenceville School Archives)

Maria and Samuel Hamill, c. 1914. In her pearl necklace, fur cape, and muff, Maria Hamill (b. 1869) sits contemplatively next to her son, Samuel Hamill III (b. 1905). Samuel was the grandson of Samuel Hamill I, who owned the Lawrenceville School (see p. 16). (Mrs. Samuel Hamill)

Lawrenceville Gothic, *c.* 1906. Frank X. (1870–1918) and Theresa Kist (1877–1988) Ketterer pose while hoeing a field at their Bunker Hill Road farm. After emigrating from Sasbach, Germany in 1883, Frank met Theresa in Trenton, where she had moved after emigrating from Obersasbach, Germany. They wed on September 6, 1891, and moved to this farm sometime after 1900. (N. Loveless)

Smiling by the fence, c. 1915. The Ketterer family and friends posing in a row for this lighthearted picture are, left to right: Ann Ketterer (cousin to Frank), unknown, Theresa Ketterer, Helen Ketterer Loveless, Eva Kist, cousin, and William Kist. (N. Loveless)

Musing with the cows, c. 1915. Leaning over the fence in the cow field are, left to right: Ann Ketterer (cousin to Frank), Theresa K. Ketterer, unknown, William Kist, Theresa H. Ketterer, Helen Ketterer, and Eva Kist. (N. Loveless)

Top, left: Field of dreams, *c.* 1915. Half hidden by the ripening ears of corn are, left to right: (front) two unknown women, Theresa H. Ketterer, William Kist, and Helen Ketterer; (back) Theresa K. Ketterer stands to the right of her daughter, Helen. Eva Kist is partially hidden by her son, William. Right: Woman with children, *c.* 1914. This unidentified woman probably worked at the Ketterer farm, where this picture was taken. She may be the mother of the children in front of her. (N. Loveless)

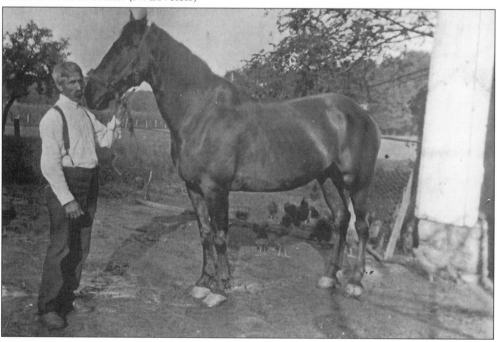

Pomona Grange, No. 5, 1914. The man in the straw boater and white shirt at the center has been tentatively identified as Thomas DeCou, a charter member of this farmer's association, or grange (see p. 26). The picture shows a meeting of Grange No. 5 at the Lawrenceville Presbyterian Church to celebrate its 50th Anniversary. The Granger Movement was begun in 1867 by farmers in Washington, DC, to protest hard times for farmers, especially high railroad shipping rates. By 1875, over 850,000 people had organized themselves in local granges across the country. Lawrence Township farmers organized the first grange in Mercer County, No. 40, P. of H., at Baker's Basin with the help of G.W. Thompson, general deputy of the National Grange. Thomas DeCou was one of the first officers. For a year No. 40 met in the Grove Schoolhouse and then built Grange Hall next to the Baker's Basin Chapel. On the first floor of the hall, the grangers opened a "co-op," a store for "co-operative buying" which saved them money by buying coal, lumber, groceries, as well as farm supplies such as seed, in large quantities. In 1877, No. 40 sent Thomas DeCou, Fannie Lukens, and E.H. Welling to the first meeting of Grange No. 5, a county-wide group. In the 1880s, as the economy improved and new laws restricted the railroads, granges closed throughout the country. In 1888 No. 40 disbanded. Grange No. 5, shown above, continued to meet well into this century. In 1907, Lawrence farmers organized another Grange, No. 170, which met twice a month above the Hullfish store and later in the new firehouse. (Lawrence Township Archives)

Opposite: Frank X. Ketterer and Starr, c. 1914. Frank holds the bridle of his horse, Starr, among the chickens in the farmyard. Four years later, Starr was hitched to the wagon when Frank suffered what may have been the first fatal traffic accident in the Township. As Frank took a load of firewood to his brother in Trenton, the wagon hit a hole in Eggert Crossing Road. The jolt threw Frank from the wagon, and he was crushed by a wagon wheel. A few days later, his wife Theresa sold their farm. (N. Loveless)

Lawrence Road firehouse, 1914/15. The Lawrenceville Volunteer Fire Association stands in front of the firehouse they built in 1914. Two lines of men pulled the hand-drawn hose carriage (foreground) to fires using the ropes held by the boy in the front, John Goulding. Their mascot sits atop the hoses piled in the carriage. The original members of the association are, left to right: (first row) Alfred Foden, Sr., unknown, Peter Ziegler, Steve Ziegler, Jr., John Hutchins, Mr. Shropshire, James Balaam, the mascot, Harry DeVaul, Charles Smith, Sr. (first chief), Bill Powner, James Ziegler, John Hulse, and Mr. Crannage; (back row) unknown, Edgar Skillman, Tom Powner, Stephen Ziegler, Sr. (first president), Elliott Poole, Al Goulding, John McCrellish, Arthur Poole, Francis Alex Crawford, Ed Whitehead, John Moulds, Alex Young, Ed Baines, and Mr. Weller. (Lawrence Township Archives)

Peerless-Rotary gear pump fire truck, 1918. The Lawrenceville Fire Company organized in 1915 with six pieces of hand-drawn equipment loaned by the Lawrenceville School. The company realized that it needed a motorized truck in order to reach fires quickly, but motorized equipment was too expensive for the volunteer company to afford. The company solved the problem by buying a 1914 Peerless automobile and a 1897 horse-drawn Silsby steam pumper. They created the truck above by installing the pumper onto the Peerless. The men in Henry Bender's wheelwright shop on Cold Soil Road then rebuilt the body of the Peerless around the new pumper. The truck was housed at the company's firehouse on Phillips Avenue, which was built in 1915. The first officers of the company were: A.G. Hullfish, president; Martin E. Carroll, vice president; George Blake, secretary; Richard W. Cook, treasurer; Urias Pierson, chief; and James E. Hullfish, assistant chief. Herman Rellstab, F.W. Kafer, and Charles J. Scott served as trustees. (B. Bentley)

Eldridge Park School, c. 1914. As the population of Eldridge Park grew after the start of the century, the Township built a new school for children in the area. This happy group is one of the first to attend the two-room school, which opened on April 1, 1913. In the back row are the school's two teachers: Irene Pycraft Rich and Mary O'Brien Cleary. (Lawrence Township Archives)

Eldridge Park School, c. 1913. Sitting in the schoolyard are John Goulding (left), the first grade teacher Mary O'Brien Cleary, and Ronald Hulse. In the background is the board fence which ran from the rear of the school to completely divide the boys' and girls' outdoor toilets to the right. (Lawrence Township Archives)

Eldridge Park School, c. 1915. This class picture shows, left to right: (front row) an unknown girl and Russ Smith; (middle row) Marquerite Seabridge, Myrtle Durling, and Gertrude Munro; (back row) John Rush, Nick Cappiello, Martha Arrison, Jim Balaam, and Edgar Smith. (Lawrence Township Archives)

Teachers, c. 1914. Standing in the Slackwood School are, left to right: (back row) Miss Hattie Bechtel, Mabel Updegrove, and Jennie Stults; (front row) Alice Nash Sailey, Mabel Sterling, and Arlene Keephart. (Lawrence Township Archives)

PUBLIC SCHOOL
ROSEDALE NOV N J 1916

Rosedale School, November 1916. The original Rosedale School was a log cabin built in the 1870s on land donated by Captain Foster W. Van Kirk, a Civil War veteran. After the school burned in the late 1800s, a new frame school was built near the site. The fields in the background of the picture above are part of the Van Kirk farm. Sitting in the center of the students is their beloved teacher, Miss Mary Virginia Hennessey, later Mrs. Malcolm Newell. At a school reunion, Mrs. Newell remembered her first day at the school. After riding from Trenton on the Johnson Trolley, walking up Cold Soil Road and opening the door, the first thing that she saw was a mouse. The boy to the far left is Alfred Cornew. To Alfred's left, Ashbrook Teeble, a "bound boy" living with the Van Kirk family, clasps Thomas B. Reed. The three boys in front on the ground are Frederick Brown, Harold "Dr." Brown, and Robert Hunt. The other students sitting around Miss Hennessy are, left to right: Louise Brown, Mary Brown, Dorothea Reed, Edna Hunt, Jennie Tyrell, Anna Tyrell, and Helen Dey, a ward of John Hill. In school, these students sat in two rows of double-seated desks with a pot-bellied stove in the center of the room. Dorothea Reed Pullen, who shared her desk with Elizabeth Drake, remembers that each desk had an inkwell that had to be checked and filled on Fridays. (Dorothea Reed Pullen)

Left: Francis J. Reed (b. 1873), *c.* 1916. Francis sits beside the hot bed in the yard of one of the homes he built on Van Kirk Road in Rosedale. The son of Mary Jane Johnson and Thomas B. Reed, Francis was a carpenter who wed Martha Ann Golden. They had five children: Philip (b. 1900), Eliza (b. 1901), Richard E. (b. 1903), Thomas B. (see p. 72), and Dorothea. Right: Dorothea Reed Pullen (b. 1910), *c.* 1918. Dorothea poses with her chicks on her shoulders and her kittens in her arms under the maple tree at her parents' Rosedale home. (Dorothea Reed Pullen)

Hullfish children, *c.* 1914. Charles Hullfish, on the left, aims his box camera at his sisters Ethel (left), and Marie, who pose with their bulldog on a crate in their backyard. (Hullfish family)

The Reeds' Tin Lizzie, c. 1917. With her friend Bonnie Moore, Dorothea Reed Pullen sits in the backseat of her father's Model-T, or "Tin Lizzie." The Reeds later owned a Studebaker, but in 1917 the car to own was the "Tin Lizzie," advertised as "the farmer's car," because it sat high enough off the ground to drive down bumpy dirt roads. Although Ford began offering Model-Ts in 1908 for $825, his mass production assembly lines allowed him to lower the price in 1912 to $575. (Dorothea Red Pullen)

Main Street, c. 1915. By 1915, cars were a frequent sight on Main Street. The car in the foreground is parked in front of the lodge. Further down the road, another car is parked in front of Applegate's. The "Garage" sign at the corner of Craven Lane was for Jim Hullfish's garage. (Lawrenceville School Archives)

Ada and Joanna Bussom, c. 1917. In this charming mother and daughter portrait, Ada and "Joy" wear the shawl collars and wide-buttoned belts that were in fashion between 1915 and 1920. The daughter of Bill Applegate (see p. 32), Ada wed Frank Bussom, who purchased the Jigger Shop (see p. 142) in 1915. (Lawrenceville School Archives)

Kennedy House, 1917. The United States entered World War I on Good Friday, April 6, 1917. The poster on the door of this student's room, "Save a loaf a week — Help win the war," refers to a wartime voluntary food conservation program. After Herbert Hoover, head of the United States Food Administration, urged families to have "Wheatless Wednesdays" to save food for the troops overseas, most Americans "saved a loaf" by eating wheatless "victory bread." Americans voluntarily did a great deal to help the war effort, such as observing "daylight saving time" to conserve fuel and planting "victory gardens" to save food. (Lawrenceville School Archives)

World War I knitting class, 1917/8. These Slackwood students helped the war effort by learning to knit socks and sweaters for the troops. The girl in the back row to the right seems to be the star pupil; she is finishing a sweater as the picture is being taken. (Lawrence Township Archives)

Raymond Arrowsmith, 1917. After the United States entered World War I, Ray enlisted in the army. He spent one and a half years as a staff sergeant with the Sixth Engineers in France building pontoon bridges across the Rhine. After being hit with mustard gas, he was discharged in 1920. (Donald Arrowsmith)

Company review, 1918. Lawrenceville School students prepared to enter World War I by organizing themselves into companies and practicing military drills. After the United States entered the War, these drills became mandatory under Major Dohm of the New Jersey National Guard. In the picture above, the French military hero Lieutenant Fourmestraux salutes the students as they stand at parade rest. Major Dohm accompanies him. Fourmestraux came to the school on April 25, 1918, to judge a review of the school's four companies. The event began at 4:15 P.M. when the companies took formation in front of the gymnasium. After marching to the golf course in formation, the lieutenant examined each company in the manual of arms. After a short drill, the companies passed in review. At 5:00 P.M., they took parade formation and stood at parade rest. The bugle corp sounded off, the colors were let down, and the companies again passed in review. The review ended with a short speech by the lieutenant, who concluded that "every moment we spend in drilling would save the life of an Allied soldier." (Hullfish family)

Company review, 1918. With the gymnasium in the background, the uniformed companies march with their guns in front of Lieutenant Fourmestraux. Forty-eight school alumni died in the war. (Hullfish family)

Company review, 1918. This overflow crowd has assembled to watch the review at the Lawrenceville School. As the school paper reported, "it seemed as if the whole Village had turned out to witness the impressive sight." (Hullfish Family)

RED CROSS HOUSE
U. S. A. Convalescent Hospital No. 1
Lawrenceville, N. J.

Red Cross hospital, c. 1918. The Red Cross ran this hospital for wounded soldiers on Lewisville Road. Along with hospital barracks for five hundred soldiers and living quarters for the doctors, the site also held a garage and a recreation building. (Hullfish family)

Red Cross nurses, 1918. Many Lawrenceville women helped the war effort by sewing shirts for the troops or nursing soldiers at the Red Cross hospital (above). During the devastating flu epidemic of 1917–19, Mary Nash (see p. 77) went to Fort Dix to nurse dying soldiers. She also held a contract to feed the soldiers that were stationed along the canal. (Lawrence Township Archives)

Red Cross soldiers, c. 1918. In the recreation building of the hospital, these uniformed soldiers relax by playing music and checkers. (Hullfish family)

Red Cross dance, c. 1918. Many local residents joined the soldiers on Lewisville Road for dances. Half hidden by the dancing couple in the center is Raymond Hullfish, Peter's (see p. 48) son. Raymond's wife, Florence Clow, stands by his side with her hands folded. (Hullfish family)

Rosedale School, 1918. This class picture shows, left to right: (front row) Elinor Blanchard, Gladys Forman, Marjorie Brown, Dorothea E. Reed, Frederick Brown, Robert W. Hunt, Harold "Dr." Brown, and Arnold Forman; (second row) Lillian McChesney, Helen Dye, Edna Hunt, Anna Tyrell, and Louise Brown; (back row) Ashbrook Teeple, Alfred Cornew, James Brown, and Thomas B. Reed. The Reed children walked 2 miles every morning to get to school, bringing their lunches in tin pails. During the lunch recess, they played games such as "Prisoner's Base" and "Giant Step." Occasionally, their teacher Miss Hennessey would join them. Most Rosedale students recalled Friday as their favorite day of the week. After a spelling bee, they would review current events and act out scenes from their reading. One student remembers marching to her seat to the music of John Phillip Souza on the victrola. If the weather was good, Miss Hennessey took them to the woods nearby to study animals, trees, and flowers. On rainy days, Miss Hennessey taught them skills such as sewing, carpentry, and caning. (Dorothea Reed Pullen)

Slackwood School, 1919. On November 7, 1918, teachers across the Township heard whistles blowing. The Board of Education sent word to each school that someone had received news of an armistice, and classes were dismissed for the day. The news turned out to be a mistake, but news of the real armistice came four days later, on November 11, 1918. Seven months later, this class graduated from the eighth grade at the Slackwood School. In this photograph are, left to right: (front row) Donovan Fagairs, Orville Flack, Julius Trossbach, Gustave Mass, Clifford Grant, and Harold Smith; (second row) Elma Nutt, Elsie Nash, Alma Scholler, Francis Rich, Gertrude Munro, Frances Swift, Jeannette Swift, Fannie Shepherd, and Leona Pancoast; (standing in back) Viola Titus and Edna Carpenter. Soon after this picture was taken, the Township renamed Rosedale Road as Carter Road in memory of Austin J. Carter, the first of three Township men to be killed in the war. (Lawrence Township Archives)

Ethel Mae Arrowsmith (1913–1935), c. 1918, and Charles H. Mather, c. 1918. Ethel, the youngest child of John and Anna Arrowsmith (see p. 100), stands next to the canal in Port Mercer. Charles Mather, posed in a bow tie and pleated shirt, owned the store shown behind Ethel. (Donald Arrowsmith)

The Fagan home, 1918. Mary Jane Johnson Reed stands with her grandson, Stewart Grayson Fagan, in front of the Greek Revival home at Port Mercer that she shared with her daughter's family. Another grandchild, Dorothea Reed Pullen, remembers covering herself in blankets for a sleigh ride from Rosedale to visit her grandmother in Port Mercer. (Dorothea Reed Pullen)

Port Mercer Airfield, *c.* 1919. These pilots are standing in an airfield on the corner of the Princeton Pike and Province Line Road. As a young boy, Edgar Updike (see p. 153) enjoyed climbing trees at his parents' home to watch the planes fly over the area. After his chores were finished, he would ride his bike down to the airfield and watch the planes take off. He remembers that the planes flew so low that one of them became ensnared in telephone wires. (Donald Arrowsmith)

Bottom, left: Port Mercer Airfield, *c.* 1919. These pilots look comfortable perched on the wooden propeller of this biplane. Right: Mary E. Dunn, *c.* 1920. In her white Mary-Janes, sailor dress, and head band, Mary poses sweetly in the backyard of her parents' Port Mercer home. (Donald Arrowsmith)

Dramatic Club, *c.* 1919. The stars of this local drama production are, left to right: (top row) Mary Hart, Jack Ryan, Kathleen Applegate, Maryann Fink, George Applegate, and Cliff Applegate; (bottom row) Walter Arrowsmith, Carrie Arrowsmith, and Margaret Applegate. (Hullfish family)

The Smith farm, *c.* 1919. William Hulse is pulling the wagon in which Ronald Hulse (left) and John Goulding sit. The Charles Smith home (see p. 11) stands on the left, and the farm outbuildings on the right. (Lawrence Township Archives)

Ice work, c. 1920. The John H. Bahrenburg Natural Ice Plant sold ice that it harvested from this pond along the Assunpink Creek at Lawrence Station. Each winter, workers opened an earthen dam to let water from the creek fill the pond. According to Mr. Bahrenburg, the Assunpink was wider and cleaner in 1920 than it is today. Before harvesting the ice, the men cleared the snow off the pond with the help of a horse, shown above. The barn in the background sports an advertisement for "Smoking Tobacco." (Lawrence Township Archives)

Storing ice "floes," c. 1920. After the snow was removed from the 17-acre pond, the men cut the ice into large squares, or "floes." They placed the "floes" on this conveyor belt, which carried them up to the 35,000-ton storage barn where the ice was insulated with sawdust and straw until it was sold the following summer. Before closing in 1926, Bahrenburg sent ice by train as far as Chicago. Mr. John H. Bahrenburg is pictured here, second from the left. (Lawrence Township Archives)

Left: At the Buxton farm, *c.* 1919. Standing on the left is Sarah Elizabeth Buxton, who bought this farm with her husband Thomas Gordon Buxton. On the right is Sarah's daughter, Betty (b. 1914), holding her *Mutt and Jeff* book. Between the Buxtons is Mrs. Glover, a neighbor. (Buxton family) Right: Port Mercer children, *c.* 1918. Posed with their dog and wagon, these children seem to be trying to stand at attention. The girl second to the left is Ethel Arrowsmith. Behind the children is the Mather home. To the right in the distance is the bridge-tender's house. (Donald Arrowsmith)

Peddler's van with woman, *c.* 1920. Even in 1920, fruit and vegetable hucksters traveled the Township selling their wares. (Lawrence Township Archives)

Five
1921–1949

Birthday party, c. 1923. Judging from the party hats they hold in their hands, these ladies seem to be assembled for a birthday party. Some of them sport the new "bob" hairstyle, with chin-length, parted hair. They all wear the new "bobbed" dresses, with scooped necks, "tubular" bodices, and pouf skirts. Shown are, left to right: (front row) unknown, Polly Pierson, Carolyn Furman, unknown, Joy Bussom, and Marjorie Smith; (middle row) Jessie Poinsett, Esther Hafner, Peg Keely, Andella Pearson, and Anna Furman; (back row) unknown, Rachael Fee, Eleanor Tilton, Jessie Johnson Reed, and unknown. (Hullfish family)

Missionary Society anniversary, *c*. 1923. To celebrate the 100th anniversary of the society, its members staged a historical pageant depicting the society's first meeting in 1821, when a group of women met at "Cherry Grove," the home of Mrs. Elizabeth Green, to form the "Lawrenceville Presbyterian Church Reading and Sewing Society." According to their 1821 constitution, they hoped to "diffuse religious intelligence throughout the community" by "sewing clothing and bedding for young ministers in Lawrenceville and the Theological Seminary at Princeton." In 1921, the society merged with the Foreign Society to become "The Women's Missionary Society of the Lawrenceville Church." Many of the members pictured above are wearing authentic nineteenth-century clothing that was handed down through their families. The women are, left to right: (seated) Miss Theodosia Johnston, Mrs. Alice Wyckoff Russull, Mrs. Lucy Sterns Prentiss, Miss Edna Wright, Mrs. Elizabeth Hendrickson Brearly, Mrs. Augusta Perrine Green, and Mrs. Mary Mershon; (standing) Mrs. Emily DeCou Tilton, Mrs. Minne Johns Stevens, Mrs. Elizabeth V. Rue, Mrs. Sarah Van Cleve Berrien, Mrs. Jeannette McPhrerson Raymond, Mrs. Hannah Shields Hendrickson, Mrs. Mary Dudley Willcox, and Mrs. Louise Berrien Grover. (Lawrenceville Presbyterian Church)

Emma Conover, c. 1923. Emma poses in the backyard of her Main Street home (see p. 43) in one of the black mourning dresses that she wore after her husband Edmund's death in 1919. Until concrete became inexpensive, many people used wooden boardwalks like the one behind Emma. Emma continued to delight Lawrenceville School boys by selling her pancakes, pies, and cookies until she was well into her eighties. She published her recipe for sponge cake in the 1926 Presbyterian Church Cookbook: "Beat 5 eggs separately. Add 1/2 pound sugar and the juice of 1 lemon. Fold 1/4 pound of flour in as lightly as possible." Presumedly, Lawrence cooks knew from these directions to "separate" the eggs and beat the whites until stiff, as well as to add the sugar and the lemon to the egg yolks before mixing them with the stiff whites. Since kitchen stoves did not have thermometers at the time, Emma does not mention the oven temperature or the cooking time. (Lawrenceville School Archives)

Watching the boats, 1921. The two boys on the left seem fascinated by this yacht gliding down the canal. (Lawrence Township Archives)

ELDRIDGE PARK GRAMMAR SCHOOL
CLASS OF 1923

Eldridge Park Grammar School, class of 1923. The boys with the armbands were members of the Lawrence Township Safety Patrol. Ronald Hulse has identified the following people in this picture of the eighth grade class: (front row) the second girl from the left is Edna Wassel, the fifth, Rosa, and the eighth, Jessie; (middle row) Bill Baker, Bill Rich, Ron Hulse, Leo Balaam, John Plant, Walt Schoeller, Walter Hutchins, Alden Baker, William Salt, and Joe King; (teachers standing in the back row) Bessie Finkel, Ethel Dettman (fourth grade), Alice B. Sailey, Esther Gaynor (kindergarten), Ethel "Pearl" Fenton (seventh grade), Mary O'Brien Cleary (music), Miss Rich, Delanna Jones Hughes, and Irene Pycraft Rich (eighth grade, then principal). Since the Township did not have its own high school until 1964, students attended high school in Trenton or Princeton, depending on whether they lived south or north of the Shabaconk Creek. The students pictured above began high school at the Junior 3 School on West State Street, Trenton. Most of these students were terrified when they arrived at school in Trenton. In Lawrence they had attended school for years with the same small group. In Trenton, their new class numbered in the hundreds. (Lawrence Township Archives)

Miss Wright's eighth grade class, 1923. Posed outside the Lawrenceville Elementary School are, left to right: (back row) Dorothea Reed Pullen, Helen Carter, Mary Wilbur, Anna Tyrell, Margaret Mertz, Honora Carroll, and Louise Brown; (front row) Edgar Updike, William Johnston, Ransom Fel, Nickolas Miller, and Joseph Wiskowkisi. (Edgar Updike)

Left: Sledding in Rosedale, c. 1925. While her sister held a quilting party in their parents' home, Dorothea Reed Pullen (center) went sledding with Hilda Burroughs (left) and May Johnson. Right: Queen Elizabeth and Walter Raliegh, c. 1927. Like her classmates (above), Dorothea Reed Pullen attended Princeton High. Here she is dressed as Queen Elizabeth for the Princeton High School Fashion Review of the Ages. (Dorothea Reed Pullen)

Davis House, 1923/4. Sitting on the right in the second row is assistant master, Thornton Wilder (1897–1975). When this picture was taken, Wilder was writing his Pulitzer Prize-winning novel, *The Bridge over San Luis Rey*. (Lawrenceville School Archives)

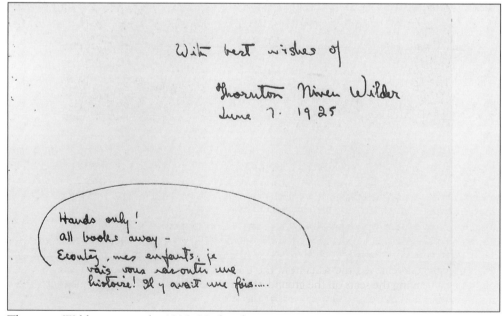

Thornton Wilder autograph, 1925. Under this signature in George A. Foye III's autograph book, Wilder wrote "Listen, my children, I will tell you a story! Once upon a time . . ." Wilder taught French at the school from 1921 to 1928. As he once explained, "There's a Wilder who loves to teach" and a "Wilder who must write novels and plays." (Lawrenceville School Archives)

Old friends, c. 1928. John H. Arrowsmith (center) seems to enjoy whittling away the time on the Port Mercer Canal bridge with his old friends William A. Howell (left) and John D. Howell. Like John, the Howells lived in the Port Mercer area all of their lives. William (b. 1858) was born in Clarksville, while John (b. 1860) was born in the Port Mercer bridge-tender's house, which at the time served as the local post office. His parents, Daniel W. and Margaret Dey Howell, moved into the house after Daniel was appointed postmaster of Port Mercer by President Abraham Lincoln. Daniel also served as the Camden and Amboy Railroad's stationmaster at Port Mercer until the depot was moved to Lawrence Station around 1867. The Howells recalled that when a troop train stopped at Port Mercer during the Civil War, the soldiers removed the seats from the train to make room for supplies. After the train pulled away leaving the seats on the ground, their mother removed the green velour upholstery from the seats and made the boys new pants out of it. (Lawrence Township Archives)

Mary Ellen "Mame" Hullfish Applegate, *c.* 1925. The long, straight, pintucked jacket, straight pleated skirt, cloched hat, pearls, and white gloves that Mary (see p. 18) wears were all elements of the "look" that became associated with the "Roaring Twenties." (Hullfish family)

Nellie Bentley Buxton, 1925. After working to save money for her passage, Nellie emigrated from Hanley, England at the age of seventeen to join her father and brother, who worked in the potteries at Millham. While vacationing with her family at a campground near the Buxton farm, she met Thomas Buxton (below). For their wedding, she wore this fashionable dress and a silk-tulle veil. (Buxton family)

Bottom, left: Thomas Buxton, c. 1923. Thomas has stopped on his bicycle for a few words with Mrs. Applegate, seated in a rocker on her front porch. Right: Kay Cook and Lyla Hullfish, c. 1925. Betty Buxton took this picture of her best friends Kay (left) and Lyla holding their dolls on the front porch of the Hullfish home. (Buxton family)

MEMBERS OF THE
Lawrence Vigilant Society

Of the Consolidated Society of New Jersey and Pennsylvania

1926

President: FRANK PIERSON   **Treasurer: RICHARD W. COOK**   **Secretary: WM. HENDRICKS**

MEMBERS:

MATHER A. ABBOTT	WALTER ELDRIDGE	CHARLES MAPLE	URIAS PIERSON
JOHN C. APPLEGATE	A. R. EVANS	EDWARD H. MAPLE	THEODORE REED
WILLIAM H. APPLEGATE	WILLIAM FARR	FRED MAPLE	A. CROZIER REEVES
JOHN ATCHLEY	E. K. FEE	HENRY MAPLE	I. RUSSELL RIKER
J. M. BERRIEN	HARRY HAFNER	WILLIAM D. MAPLE	CHARLES N. RISDON
MARTIN E. CARROLL	HENRY HAFNER	DELMAR MERRITT	H. ARTHUR SMITH
WALTER CARSON	JOHN B. HARRIS	JOSEPH W. MILLER	CHARLES H. SMITH
JESSE COLEMAN	FRANK HENDRICKSON	ALFRED PIERSON	J. L. STOUT
RICHARD W. COOK	JACOB L. HENDRICKSON	CHARLES PIERSON	STANLEY TERHUNE
IRVING COOPER	WILLIAM HENDRICKSON	EDGAR H. PIERSON	FRED C. UPDYKE
M. R. DAWLEY	J. AUGUSTUS HULIT	FRANK PIERSON	ARTHUR VAN CLEVE
ALBERT DECOU	A. G. HULLFISH	J. GOLDEN PIERSON	GEORGE W. VAN KIRK
GEORGE DRAKE	JAMES E. HULLFISH	LEWIS D. PIERSON	JOHN S. VAN KIRK
WILLIAM DUMONT	PETER S. HULLFISH	ORMAND PIERSON	EDGAR G. WEART
RAYMOND DYE	FRANK JOHNSON	RANDOLPH PIERSON	GEORGE S. WHITE
OSCAR EGGERT	PHILLIP H. JOHNSON	THEODORE PIERSON	DUDLEY WILLCOX

Lawrence Vigilant Society placard, 1926. Behind the names on this membership list lies one of the more interesting chapters in the history of law enforcement in New Jersey. The first law enforcement group in the Township, as in many New Jersey towns, was a vigilant society, a group of local property owners who organized to seek justice for property crimes such as theft or arson. State law authorized incorporated vigilant societies to "apprehend and arrest upon view and without warrent, any person committing breaches of peace" and "bring them before a Justice of Peace . . . to be dealt with according to law." In New England, similar groups had existed since 1800. The society was informally known as a "horse company," because if a crime occurred that caused at least $10 in damage to a member's property, the president and directors of the society would assign men called "pursuers" to chase the suspect on horseback, sometimes over 50 miles. The assignments and routes were kept secret. The "pursuers" had to keep riding until the president sent word that they could stop, or pay a fine to the society. The society initially elected twenty "pursuers." By 1916, the society began protecting cars as well as horses. After the state police began patrolling Lawrence in 1922 and the municipal police force in 1924, the society began meeting simply as a social group until it disbanded in 1942. (Lawrence Township Archives)

Left: Vigilant society badge, *c.* 1926. George Vankirk gave Lieutenant William Hullfish this badge, the only "detective" badge worn by a vigilant society member now known to exist. (Lawrence Township Archives) Right: Senator Crozer Reeves (1867–1936), *c.* 1925. One member of the vigilant society was Senator Reeves, president of *The Trenton Times* newspaper and four term state senator. As senator, he sponsored legislation to double the strength of the state police, to reduce the state budget, and to establish free toll bridges. (Raymond Updike)

Walter Arrowsmith, *c.* 1922. When the state police was formed in 1922, it patrolled on horseback. Walter is pictured in his state police uniform after passing vigorous tests in riding and jumping to qualify for the force. He was killed in a motorcycle accident while on duty in 1926. (Donald Arrowsmith)

The Deacon Entangled, March 9/10, 1926. The Rosedale Men's Club sponsored The Rosedale Players' performances of this comedy by Harry Osborne. The members of the cast and their roles in the play were, from left to right: Margaret "Peggy" Schilling as Dr. Sopher's daughter; Henry Rigley Jr. as Calvin Spangler; Kyle McWhester as Harry Baxter; Dorothea Reed Pullen as Ruth Baxter; E.T. "Ed" House as Reverend Dr. Sopher; Marion Vaudewater Naumann as Mrs. Penrose; Lillian Vandewater as the maid; Paul Hill (seated) as Deacon Penrose; Harold Blackwell as both the policeman and the plainclothes man. In these days before television, plays were a popular form of entertainment. People enjoyed socializing at play rehearsals as much as they enjoyed watching a production. In Rosedale, plays were performed at the Rosedale Chapel, the local center of activity. During the week, many people tied up their horses at the chapel and then took the Johnson Trolley to work. On weekends, various groups organized church socials and variety shows at the chapel, though never dances. Eliza Reed remembers rope tricks being performed at one variety show by an Indian from Carlisle, Pennsylvania, who worked at a local farm. (Dorothea Reed Pullen)

Left: Charles Gilpin, c. 1920. Charles appears in his costume for the starring role in Eugene O'Neill's *Emperor Jones*. After Paul Robeson took over the part, Charles retired to Eldridge Park where he died in 1930.Right: George Emerson Applegate, c. 1929. George, the son of William Applegate (see p. 32), won many athletic awards in school and later became a coach at the Hun School and the Peddie School. (Lawrence Township Archives)

Daily Vacation Bible School, 1927. Many Township children enjoyed this summer school, which was founded by the Lawrenceville Presbyterian Church in 1925. Sitting in the front row are the school administrators: Louise Mass, Reverend Parke Richards, Jr., Helen Carter, and Reba Poinsett. (Lawrence Township Archives)

"Pop" Bussom, *c.* 1929. After he bought the Jigger Shop in 1915, Frank "Pop" Bussom presided at the counter instead of Al (see p. 46). "Pop" pours the jigger topping into a paper cup rather than a glass, but lunchtime in Lawrenceville still meant a jigger. (Lawrence Township Archives)

The Jigger Shop, 1929. Standing in their white jackets behind the marble counter in the Jigger Shop are, left to right: Ralph Saunders, Ray Arrowsmith, Jim West, Reba Poinsett, and Pop Bussom. Ralph holds a jigger scoop and cup up for the camera. (Lawrence Township Archives)

Outside the Jigger Shop, 1929. By 1927, the Jigger Shop's business had grown so much that "Pop" moved it from Kafer Flats to this large building across the street. The new shop had a dining room (right), as well as a counter. Posing outside the shop are, left to right: Ralph Sanders, Pop Bussom, Ray Arrowsmith, and Jim West. Ray began working at the shop in 1915 when "Pop" asked Ray's parents if he and his brother George could work in the shop before and after school (see p. 100). They agreed, and the two boys moved in with the Bussoms to begin work at the store. Although George left the shop in 1925, Ray stayed and eventually bought the shop from "Pop" in 1948. Over the years, Ray and "Pop" became good friends, even though "Pop" did play a number of practical jokes on Ray. "Pop" was known throughout the Village for his practical jokes. The night he was married, his friends decided to even the score by giving him a "Shivaree," a rowdy surprise party for newlyweds. One of the partygoers, A.G. Hullfish, told his son Bill (see p. 145) that after the party arrived at Bussom's, some of them kept "Pop" busy going outside to the cider barrels for refills. In the meantime, the others re-assembled the beds on the porch roof. When "Pop" re-appeared in the Village after a few days, he said that only one of the jokes had really bothered him — when he put on his work shoes the next morning, his feet had gotten covered with "foot-ease." Apparently, "foot-ease" was "Pop's" way of saying that someone had taken his shoes to the barn and filled them with manure. The Student's Pressing Shop, to the left of the Jigger Shop above, was owned by A.G. and Peter Coffee. The Pressing Shop did a brisk business, because the strict dress code at the Lawrenceville School required the students to keep a large supply of clean shirts and pressed suits. The post office is on the far left (see p. 153). (Lawrence Township Archives)

Chief Joseph Leland Hopkins, *c.* 1929. After serving as a truant officer and the Township's first full-time police officer, Joseph Hopkins was sworn in as the first police chief in 1924. He sits on the motorcycle he used to patrol the Township until the force began using cars in 1929. (Lawrence Township Archives)

Recorder's court, *c.* 1929. Standing in front of the Township recorder's, or crimina,l court at Harney's Corner are, left to right: Officer D. Ackroyd, Officer G. Bond, Court Clerk John W. Toft, Recorder Edwin Carpenter, Police Chief Hopkins, Police Commissioner George Turner, Police Officer Joseph Stonicker, and Officer G. Wood. Everyone on the force was on call twenty-four hours a day. (Lawrence Township Archives)

144

Crime scene, c. 1930. Chief Hopkins (right) helps funeral directors Frank (center) and Walter (left) Swaze load a wicker casket into an undertaker's van. The scene has not been identified. It could be that of a still blowing up, one of the few fatal accidents during this time. (Lawrence Township Archives)

William Hullfish, c. 1934. Bill, the son of A.G. and Etta Hullfish (see p. 68), had this portrait taken for his graduation from high school. After marrying Florence Stein, he served on the Township police force for thirty-six years. (Hullfish family)

Nellie the Man, *c.* 1932. Standing in front of the garage on the Buxton Dairy farm are, left to right: Mr. Sartor, "Nellie the Man," and Richard Buxton. Nellie wears the latest in men's fashion: felt hat, spectacles, and overcoat. Nellie's owner, Betty Buxton (see p. 128), has enjoyed many pets over the years, from dogs and lambs to turkeys and java rice birds. (Buxton family)

Left: Thomas and Gordon Buxton, *c.* 1931. Thomas (see p. 137) holds his son Gordon, who seems eager to try out this handknit suit in a walk around the Buxton farm. The dairy truck in the background reads "Buxton's Dairy, GrAde Pasturized Heavy Cream." Right: Billie Morton and Nellie the dog, *c.* 1931. After helping Billie pick a bouquet of daisies, Nellie appears here as herself. The building in the background served as the milk house at the farm. (Buxton family)

Griswold vs. Raymond, c. 1931. This picture captures the various looks on the players' faces just as a play had ended during this interhouse game. The boys in the striped uniforms seem pleased with the outcome of the play. (Lawrenceville School Archives)

Coffee at Dickinson House, c. 1938. Continuing Samuel Hamill's tradition of entertaining students in the parlor (see p. 16), Mrs. Theodore H. Keller graciously serves coffee to the residents of Dickinson House. Mr. Keller, the house master, was the school organist. (Lawrenceville School Archives)

AT&T transatlantic short-wave radio station, *c.* 1931. Before the first transatlantic telephone cable was laid across the Atlantic Ocean in 1956, phone calls were sent overseas by radio waves. After successfully testing an overseas short-wave radio transmission in 1928, AT&T opened a permanent transatlantic short-wave radio station on Cold Soil Road in June 1929. All the overseas telephone calls in the United States were sent overseas from Cold Soil Road. Calls from overseas were received at another station in Netcong, New Jersey. The main building at the 840-acre site (above) housed offices and transmitters, as well as equipment to prepare the voice current for transmission. Because of its high-voltage equipment, the site was not open to the public. Residents throughout the Township wondered what was happening at the site. People were especially concerned about the radio towers, such as the ones in back of the main building above. From a distance, the twelve 180-foot-high towers, each with five red lights, looked like a mile-long building. Rumors flew about the huge building on the hill. The reality was much simpler than what people imagined. After a person asked the operator to make an overseas call, the operator routed the call through an office in New York City to Lawrenceville. In the main building at Lawrenceville (above), a current set up in the telephone wire by the voice of the caller entered the "line terminal room" (opposite), where technicians adjusted their equipment to suit the call. From there, the voice was carried to the transmitter room. Here, the voice current entered a modulator where it was blended with a high frequency current so that it could be transmitted through air. This current traveled outside into one of the twelve antennae, which sent it into the air in the right direction as a radio wave. Once overseas, the process was repeated in reverse. A three minute call from New York to England cost $45. (Newark Library)

AT&T line terminal room, c. 1929. D.B. McKey (left), technical employee, and H.T. Ashworth, radio man, sit at the testboard where they prepare the voice current to be transformed into a radio wave. To prevent the energy from the antennae outside from disrupting the testboard circuitry, the entire room was swathed in sheet copper, the windows with copper mesh. (Newark Library)

Rosedale School reunion, 1931. These alumni gather in front of the school during one of their annual reunions. Civil War veteran Peter Van Kirk sits to the far left of the middle row with his hat on his knee. The two men in the center of the front row are Mr. Golden (left) and Uriah Pierson. (Lawrence Township Archives)

Rosedale School reunion, 1931. This close-up of the alumni shows Randolph Pierson standing on the left. Lu Silcox stands in the back row to the far right. George Van Kirk stands on the right in the second row from the back. To his right is Walter Van Kirk. In front of Walter is Francis J. Reed. Hilda Pierson, a teacher, stands third from the left in the second row to the back. (Lawrence Township Archives)

An Arrowsmith family reunion, *c.* 1933. The members of the Arrowsmith family shown above include: John, Anne, Fannie, Carrie, Ethel, and Dink Arrowsmith; Mr. and Mrs. Ray Arrowsmith; Mr. and Mrs. George Arrowsmith and their son Walter; Mr. and Mrs. Josh Bilderback; Elaine Seely; Mae Seely; Mr. Elizabeth McKensie; Mr. and Mrs. George Hutchinson; Mr. and Mrs. Carl Luker; Mr. and Mrs. Clark Arrowsmith; Mr. and Mrs. William Titus and their daughters Helen and Viola; Mr. and Mrs. Clifford Allen; Clarence Allen; John and Annie Arrowsmith; Mr. and Mrs. Isaac Groendyke; Thaddus Kurts. (Donald Arrowsmith)

Hafner's Place, *c.* 1935. This Texaco station on the north side of Route 206 sold leaded gasoline for16¢ a gallon. The signs on the steeple guaranteed that motorists would have plenty of time to slow down before reaching the store. Some of the other signs on the building advertised ice cream, fresh eggs, soft drinks, and ice. (Lawrence Township Archives)

The daughter of Mr. and Mrs. William F. Tilton (see p. 86), Edith Branson Tilton, stands in her parents' home, just before she married Raymond Updike, the son of Mr. and Mrs. Edgar Updike, in 1933. The long, lean lines of her dress show how 1930s fashions moved away from the dropped waists and pleated skirts of the 1920s. Raymond, his father, and his brother decorated the Presbyterian Church with fresh fir trees (right), so that the ceremony would be swathed in the fragrance of pine. (Raymond Updike)

The Edith Tilton/Ray Updike wedding, 1933. With their parents' support, Edith and Raymond were one of the first couples to brave the Depression and get married. Edith and Raymond sit proudly in the front row. Raymond's brother Edgar, standing in back of him, served as the best man. (Raymond Updike)

Taking aim, *c.* 1938. Snowball in hand, Charles Hullfish sits in front of the No. 4 school on a truck from his uncle A.G. Hullfish's business, The Lawrenceville Ice and Coal Company. A.G. had started the business by selling ice that he harvested from a pond on the Rouse farm (see p. 70) to local families, who needed ice for their iceboxes. In 1925, the company began selling coal as well as ice. As refrigerators replaced iceboxes in the 1930s, the company began selling fuel oil and installing fuel burners. In 1948, the company stopped selling ice completely. (Hullfish family)

Post office, 1937. Even in the 1930s, the Lawrenceville Post Office served as a town meeting hall. The postal employees standing in front of the building are, left to right: George Coffee, clerk; Martin E. Carroll, postmaster; an unknown mail carrier; Ray Hauck, Lawrenceville School mail carrier; Edgar Updike, clerk. (Edgar Updike)

Pageant, c. 1937. Performing in this historical pageant in the Furman's living room (see p. 59) are, left to right: Marie Hullfish Hulit, Jessie Johnston Reed, unknown, Polly Pierson, and Miss Havens. (Hullfish family)

Building St. Anne's, August 1937. Giuseppe Pilla (front) guides the earth scoop that is digging the basement of St. Anne's Roman Catholic Church on Lawrenceville Road. Many local families helped build the church: the Pillas, the Cermeles, the Simonellis, the Colavitas, the Constantinis, the Pasquitos, the DiSylvesters, the D'Amico's, and the Kites. Even Father McCorristin was often found covered with dirt on the building site. Joseph Cermele, the son of Emily and Andrew, was the first baby baptized in the church. (Lawrence Township Archives)

Eldridge Park baseball field, Eldridge Park, *c.* 1937. Baseball was Eldridge Park's favorite sport, and Slackwood (below) its main rival. Relaxing between innings are Sal Pasquito, Dan DiSylvester, and Jim Smith. (Lawrence Township Archives)

Slackwood baseball team, *c.* 1940. The team, the coaches, and in the front, the batboys, pose for this team picture at the field on the Princeton Pike. The man seated in the center seems to be "Pop" Candles, who worked at the Slackwood School. (Lawrence Township Archives)

The Updike family, *c.* 1936. While the children sit waiting for a shower in tubs on the front lawn, Edith Updike and her friend chase the dog, Jack, who seems completely unwilling to go near the water. (Raymond Updike)

Left: Gertrude Scudder (1860–1944), *c.* 1940. Gertrude was a talented organist who delighted members of the Lawrenceville Presbyterian Church with her playing for forty years. She lived at Cherry Grove with her husband, Joseph Rue Scudder, until 1910. (Raymond Updike) Right: Donald Schenck Anderson, May 1940. The son of Dury and Georgianna Schenck Anderson, Donald sits on Lewisville Road in front of his parents' home. The Schenck family were charter members of the Mt. Pisgah A.M.E. Church (see p. 32) across the road from Donald. (Lawrence Township Archives)

Slackwood graduating class, 1941. Although these students still wear the same kind of suits and dresses as their parents, they have adopted a different style of footwear: bobby socks and saddle shoes. Over the next twenty years, this small difference in footwear would grow into an entirely new teen fashion industry. Shown are, left to right: (front row) Marion Clark, Eleanor Graf, Dorothy Jones, Marion Applegate, John Reading, Roy Sellinberger, Joan Gratton, Gene Miller, Iris Rice, Jane Wilcox, and Dorothy Krause; (second row) James Coxon, Francis Daufters, Alice Shaw, Harriet Arnold, Miss Updegrove, Irene Coan, Margaret Laske, Leonard Chale, Kenneth Bowers, and Bruce Campbell; (third row) Fred Majeski, Walter Robins, Richard Toft, Joseph Nadoney, Carl Elder, and Howard Alrich. (Lawrence Township Archives)

EMS charter members, 1947. The members of the first Township Emergency Squad posing in front of the Municipal Building (see p. 55) are, left to right: (front row) Jim Eaton, Jack Maple, Fred Bentley, Tom Hawthorn, Ed Friman, and Harold Edwards; (back row) Jim Tucker, Frank Buxton, Gordon Buxton, Bill Walter, Vince Terranova, Fred Ettenger, Carl Summers, and Don Baker. Captain Tony Pilla stands in front of the sleek ambulance. Two other members, Al Alden and S. Stanzione, were absent for this photograph. (Lawrence Township Archives)

Route 1, c. 1945. This view looking north on Route 1 shows the Shipetaukin Creek bridge on the left in the foreground. The bridge in the distance spans the canal. Route 1 was expanded from two to four lanes in the 1930s. (Lawrence Township Archives)

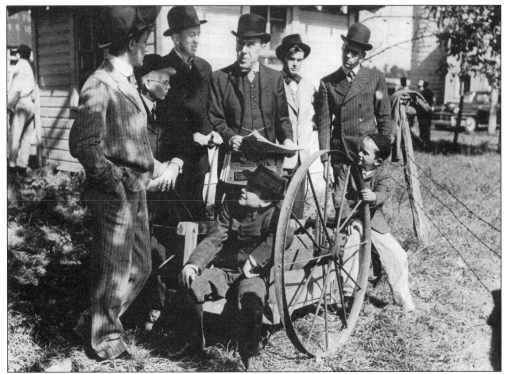

The Happy Years, September 1949. When film crews invaded Lawrence to film *The Happy Years*, a movie based on Owen Johnson's stories, one resident described it "like a circus, only better." Movie stars, lights, and cameras were everywhere. A number of local boys were even hired as extras at $10 a day. Here stand extras Charles Hullfish, Jr., Jimmy Souter, Leo J. Carroll (who played "The Roman," see p. 43), Victor Rosner, and John Maple. William Hullfish (left) and Robert Hullfish sit on the horsecart. (Hullfish family)

The Happy Years, September 1949. William (left) and Robert Hullfish wait in a horsecart to join a parade of seventeen carriages down Blackwell Road for a scene involving a ride to the Lawrenceville School. They sit with George Chandler, who played their Great Uncle Jimmy Hullfish (see p. 96). The film's director, William A. Wellman, paid Robert to serve as a security guard and keep people away from the director's chair. (Hullfish family)

Select Bibliography

Amory, Cleveland. Introduction to *The Lawrenceville Stories*, by Owen Johnson. New York: Simon and Schuster, 1967.

Everts and Stewart. *Combination Atlas Map of Mercer County*. Philadelphia, 1875.

Lawrence Historic and Aesthetic Commission. *Volume I of the Minutes of Lawrence (Maidenhead) Township*. Trenton: Spruce Printing Company, 1976.

Phillips, George. Diary. Lawrence Township Archives. Mercer County Library, Lawrence Township.

Podmore, Harry J., ed. *The Presbyterian Church of Lawrenceville, New Jersey*. Princeton: Princeton University Press, 1948.

Reeder, Ella Elizabeth. Letter to Mrs. Reeder, November, 1864. Lawrence Township Archives. Mercer County Library, Lawrence Township.

Seymour, John. *The Forgotten Crafts*. New York: Alfred A. Knopf, 1984.

Slaymaker, S.R. *Five Miles Away: The Story of the Lawrenceville School*. Princeton: Princeton University Press, 1985.

Tanner, Mary C. *A Different World: An Oral History of Lawrenceville, New Jersey*. Lawrenceville: The Presbyterian Church of Lawrenceville, 1992.

Tyler, Donald H. *Old Lawrenceville: Early Houses and People*. N. p.: 1965.

Woodward, Major E.M. and Hageman, John F. *History of Burlington and Mercer Counties, New Jersey, with Biographical Sketches of Many of their Pioneers and Prominent Men*. Philadelphia, 1883.